THE CRY OF MY PEOPLE
Out of Captivity in Latin America

Esther and Mortimer Arias

The Lord said,
    I have seen the affliction of my people
            who are in Egypt.
    I have heard *the cry of my people*
            Against their slave-masters.
I have taken heed of their sufferings, and
    I have come down to deliver them
            out of the hands of the Egyptians,
            to bring them out of that country,
            to a good and broad land,
            a land flowing with milk and honey. . . .

Exodus 3:7-8

Friendship Press
New York

About the Artist

Walter Solón Romero is a muralist who in 1961 won Bolivia's National Art Prize. Well-known in international art circles, Romero has had his work displayed in nearly all the capitals of the world.

In the city of Sucre Romero founded a group of artists and intellectuals, called "Anteo," which became Bolivia's first school for muralists. Its members have strongly influenced contemporary Bolivian painting.

Romero studied at the Escuela de Bellas Artes and the Escuela Nacional de Maestros in Bolivia and later at the Faculty of Plastic Arts of the University of Chile and at the Engraving Workshop of the Museum of Modern Art in Rio de Janeiro. He continued his studies with UNESCO projects in Japan, India, Egypt and Greece.

His art is a personal witness (his own son was tortured and killed in prison) of "the cry of my people" in the last decade of captivity.

Library of Congress Cataloging in Publication Data

Arias, Esther, 1923–
    The cry of my people.

    Includes bibliographical references.
    1. Latin America—Social conditions—1945-2. Latin America—Economic conditions—1945-3. Church and social problems—Latin America. 4. Liberation theology. I. Arias, Mortimer, joint author. II. Title.
HN110.5.A8A63   980'.03   80-11426
ISBN 0-377-00095-7

Editorial Offices: 475 Riverside Drive, New York, NY 10027
Distribution Offices: P. O. Box 37844, Cincinnati, OH 45237

CONTENTS

"Don Quixote, with doves of hope confusing the attacking dogs" by Solōn.

FOREWORD

The Cry of My People sounds an alert, uttering a cry of the heart that calls for responsive openness, discernment and self-searching. It challenges North American Christians to understand the social, economic and political realities of Latin America—often in relation to North American involvement—and the perspectives, sensitivities and theological and political motivations of many Christians in that populous region.

In coming to these pages, the reader should keep in mind, among others, at least four interrelated realities.

First, authors Esther and Mortimer Arias rightly place Latin America in the Third World. With but several exceptions, the common factor among Third World nations is their past experience of Western colonialism. Some still feel today economic, technological or political domination from the West and designate it neo-colonialism. Yet less widely recognized, the Third World also contains millions of Christians who carry a large and growing share in the life of the church.

Despite the varied definitions given to the Third World, the authors employ it in its most widely used form to designate the lands and peoples of Asia and the Pacific (2.5 + billion), Africa (460 million) and Latin America (375 million). The Third World's 3.35 billion people, of whom some 650 + million (19.5 percent) are Christians, constitute 77 percent of the world's population. The old "European Christendom"—from Russia, through Europe and Northern America, and across to Australia and New Zealand—numbers 1.02 billion people, of whom some 650 million (64 percent) are Christians, and represents 23 percent of the global population. Put simply, those 1.3 + billion Christians constitute 30 percent of the world's 4.37 billion people.

More importantly, those figures point to two larger considerations. First, the task of world evangelization grows steadily. Second, a new reality has emerged in universal and Christian history. Numerically, Christians in the Third World now slightly exceed—and in twenty years, by 2000 A.D. will considerably exceed—those in the West. The universal gospel now demonstrates its universality. The world today can identify Christianity's presence among every part of God's human family. As in past major transitions, Christianity's center of gravity is shifting decisively.

God's mission abides. Yet, as Christianity in the Third World attests, the missions of God's covenanted people are in process of massive transition. The view of that transition from Latin America provides the setting for this book.

As a second consideration, one notes that the unchanging gospel finds varied forms of expression in different settings and eras. When transplanted, it reflects in part the coloration of its new environment. When renewed, it addresses new concerns. Either process involves debate and struggle. In either, some hold that others, in trying to express the gospel in ways appropriate to the culture and the needs of people, distort the gospel. This pattern has occurred many times, but can be illustrated best, even without developing clarifying details, within Christianity's three major transitions.

The first began in Paul's day with the transplantation of the gospel from its Jewish and Palestinian base to that of the Greco-Roman World with its quite different philosophical outlook. The second emerged with the fall of the Western Roman Empire in 476. The greek influence continued in Eastern Orthodoxy. Yet in the Latin West missionary monks won the barbarians and, in the process between 500 and 1500 A.D., the papacy, princes and people created Europe.

Meanwhile, Christianity on the Iberian Peninsula (Spain and Portugal) engaged in an eight-century encounter with the Muslim conquerors and Islam. There the fusion of church and state under the papacy brought reconquest through crusade and inquisition. The result? The spirit of vigorous encounter remained and a unique expression of the faith emerged—Iberian Catholicism. The fall of Granada in 1492 ended the reconquest and Iberian Catholicism then became a factor in the conquest and life of Latin America.

The events of that period conveniently mark the beginning of the gospel's third great transplantation to the Americas and Asia, to Africa and the Pacific. The Iberians led in the sixteenth century. Others followed, and finally in the nineteenth century Protestants moved vigorously into world mission. The legacy of that mission includes Christianity's remarkable growth in the Third World *and* a world Christian community. The gospel now finds expression through all the rich and diverse gifts with which God has endowed humanity.

A third point bears noting. Today the whole world is caught up in a universal history. Within it, history itself is viewed as linear and purposive, not cyclical and meaningless. In it human beings can claim worth and dignity. Determination to achieve a better life has swept away the old fatalisms. Even the monstrous distortions of human rights and a readiness by some to destroy millions or imprison multitudes, supposedly to facilitate a better life for those to follow, bear a fiendishly warped testimony to the power of the ultimate goal.

Whether recognized or not, this view of purposive history and of human worth roots in the Christian gospel and also discloses the gospel's work in all humankind beneath the tides of history. This dynamic generates the drive for justice, equality, freedom, and liberation from any bondage destroying hope and life. The United Nations' 1948 Universal Declaration of Human Rights, so widely affirmed in the Third World, sinks its taproot into the same source. In Latin America the same dynamic today challenges the indigenous Indian religions that attached itself to the region's "old Catholicism."

Fourth and finally, a new religious vitality moves across Latin America. After 450 years there, the Roman Catholic Church was lethargic and seemed impotent, still depended upon Europe for more than half its clergy, and had linked itself with the ruling elites. Yet in that church the past 25 years have brought striking change. Greatly stimulated by Vatican II (1962-65), its bishops in 1968 affirmed the "re-evangelization" of the whole region and allied themselves and the church with the hopes of the impoverished masses for justice and a better life. In the process, vigorous new life at the grass-roots animates the laity. Protestantism, too, and notably through Pentecostalism, contributes to this awakening.

In short, four factors meet in this book: the important multi-voiced Christian reality in the Third World; the transplantation/renewal factor that articulates the gospel in new and often controversial ways; the purposive dynamic of universal history with its imperative for human dignity; and a religious renaissance. They point to its larger context and importance.

The authors' account is moving, provocative and revealing. Reflect on it thoughtfully. Read further for clarity. If at some points you disagree, ask questions, or take issue knowledgeably. Finally, determine what authentic, concerned Christian response means or could mean to this "cry of the people." If you so enter the dialogue into which the authors invite you, both they and you will have gained. Quite possibly an even larger community may benefit.

—W. Richey Hogg, Professor of World Christianity, Perkins School of Theology, Southern Methodist University, Dallas, Texas

PREFACE

Why study Latin America? For Christian readers of the United States of America and Canada there are three obvious answers: 1) because what happens to our neighbors south of the Rio Grande affects us all; 2) because in Latin America today Christianity is at stake, and Christian mission is on the verge of a radical turn in its history; 3) because as Christians we are called to love and care for all persons, so we need to know them better.

A few years ago, several church mission boards in the United States sponsored a task force on Latin America whose conclusions were published in a booklet entitled, *Latin America: Illusion or Reality?* It begins with this picture:

> South from us a hemisphere is appearing, a giant is beginning to awaken, to rise up, to look around, to feel hungry and to stretch his muscles. Latin America, a land of great beauty and incredible poverty, the land of a small and shining leading class and of a vast, oppressed and exploited peasant class. And interwoven in the Latin American fabric are the "Yankees"—tourists, military, businessmen, wealthy North Americans possessing great private real estate and powerful companies with great operations in Latin America. And the missionaries.[1]

Latin America, with a territory of seven million square miles, similar to the United States and Canada together, is a growing giant. From a population of 200 million in 1950, it has reached 350 million in 1980, and it will have 600 million in the year 2000. Canada and the United States, with a present total population of 230 million, will have 312 million at the end of the century.

In spite of all our differences, all of us in the American continent are literally "in the same boat." A few of us travel first class, many of us second or third class, but millions of us are living in the galleys of this continental boat. A few are on the deck or in the commander's room, some are in the machine room, others enjoy themselves in the restaurant or the dance hall. But no matter what our position, our income, our diet, or our entertainment may be, all of us are in the same boat—we will sail together or we will sink together. While we ride the waves on this huge *Titanic* of the Americas, to ignore each other is a non-permissible, suicidal luxury.

The last decade has been hard on our people south of the Rio Grande, in political frustrations, economic exploitation, social oppression and military and police repression. We have been living in captivity in our own land! As in biblical times, a new theology has been born from our exile and out of our captivity—the theology of liberation. We have been rediscovering the God of Exodus, the Liberating God. Out of the depths of oppression and repression we may have something to share with Christians of the North, something of what the Lord has been saying to us throughout this dreadful experience.

The Cry of My People

"I have *heard* the cry of my people," said the Lord to Moses. The first and decisive revelation of God in the Bible is that God cares for people who suffer, for little people, for slaves, for the poor and oppressed. This God is not up there on Olympus, like the Greek gods. He descends to the depths of our condition and our suffering. He is not deaf or blind or indifferent: "I have *seen* the affliction of my people who are slaves. . . . I *know* their suffering and I have *come down to deliver* them out of the hands of the Egyptians, and to bring them out to a good and broad land, a land flowing with milk and honey. . . . Come, I will send you to Pharaoh that you may *bring forth my people*" (Exodus 3:7-10; 6:5-8).

Christians in Latin America are beginning to hear "the cry of my people." Consequently, they are beginning to know better the Liberating God of the Bible and to recognize the incarnate Christ in the faces of the suffering poor. Facing the inhuman conditions of the people of the northeast of Brazil, some Catholic bishops felt like Moses in the face of his people's intolerable slavery and tried to respond to God's liberating call in a similar way. They said in a now famous document:

These words from Exodus, spoken by God to Moses, are a fitting expression of our feelings in these days (Exodus

3:11-12; 4:12). Before the suffering of our people, humble and oppressed for centuries, we feel called by the Word of God to take up a position, a clear position on the side of the poor, a position taken in common with all those who commit themselves to people for their true liberation.

Following in the steps of Moses, we want to fulfill, together with the people of God, our mission as pastors and prophets. We are summoned to speak by the Word of God, which judges the events of history. In this way we have tried to understand the cry of our people, the daily facts and events of a suffering people—phenomena which recommend themnselves to a serious study of our human situation.

In the awareness of our frequent omissions and uncertainties in the course of the history of our Church . . . we feel powerless and awed before such a huge task. We spontaneously repeat the question asked of Yahweh by Moses: "Who am I that I should go to Pharaoh?" But we also feel a strength from above, the grace of the One who has called and sent us: "God answered: I will be with you. . . . Go, and I will be your mouth and teach you what you shall speak."[2]

The ecumenical group from the United States and Canada who decided to publish this book were trying to attempt "a serious study of our human situation in Latin America" by raising some of the most significant issues of the Latin America situation and calling the attention of the Christians and churches in the northern hemisphere to them.

Let us hope that through the following pages, which come from the experience of captivity in Latin America during the last 10 years, you may also hear with us "the cry of my people." And that, with God's help, you may share in responding to their struggle for total liberation, according to God's purpose for his people.

1

WHERE IS MY NEIGHBOR?
Behind Facts and Figures

Awareness, identification, responsible action: Quite a challenge for Christians who care! But how can we become aware? Are facts and figures enough? The sponsors of this book hope that this study may help North American Christians to identify with oppressed people and, in understanding other people's values, to understand also their own cultural value systems and political and economic assumptions. Transcultural exchanges often help people gain such an understanding. But how can you identify with people who live in a strikingly different world? How can you understand oppressed people without sharing their lot? How far can we go in our identification? And how can our response be adequate without awareness and identification of some sort?

The first step is to become *aware*, like the Good Samaritan, who saw the man on the road. The priest and the Levite also saw him, but they "passed by on the other side." They were aware of the stripped, beaten, half-dead man on the road, but they did not *identify* with him and they did not *respond* with the necessary deed. They did not recognize him as a "neighbor." They did not become his "neighbor."

To identify with your neighbor you need *empathy*—feeling with the other, putting yourself in the place of the other. The Samaritan, "when he saw him he had *compassion*." Moreover, you have *to cross to the other side of the road*—to cross barriers. The Samaritan crossed the road and "went to him." In those few steps he crossed racial, religious and social barriers that separated a Samaritan from a Jew (Luke 10: 29-37). *To respond is to cross barriers.*

So, to identify ourselves with the oppressed, we have to cross boundaries. Gustavo Gutiérrez, the Peruvian theologian of liberation, has said that to serve Christ in the neighbor, as Jesus in the Gospel

1

(Matthew 25: 31-46) told us to do, we have to cross from "our world" to the "world of the other" in whom Christ is waiting for us. To love our neighbor does not mean only to love the neighbor "near me," the individual that comes my way. It means also to love the "faraway," the "distant" neighbor who belongs to a different class, race, sex, group or nation. It is the neighbor who belongs to the oppressed and faceless masses whose world I have to enter, with whose cause I have to side. This is not an easy thing to do. It demands, in fact, a truly "evangelical conversion"—*the conversion to Christ in the neighbor*. This conversion is much more than an intellectual, detached, objective knowledge about my neighbor. It is a real movement from my world to the world of "the other."[1] This is what conversion means: a turning around—to God in the neighbor.

If, then, to identify and to respond amounts to a real conversion, we obviously cannot expect to accomplish this by only reading a book. Although, in God's grace, the call to conversion may resound through these pages and, through the work of the Spirit, many may respond to it. We hope, though, that what is about to be studied may help to remind ourselves that *our neighbor is there*—behind facts and figures. If we are sensitive enough, we may even hear "the cry of my people" coming from below the abstract figures and the bare facts.

Who Is My Neighbor? A Christian

My neighbor is a Christian.

Of the 350 million Latin Americans, 90 to 95 percent consider themselves Christians. Of course, not all nominal Christians will be practicing Christians or, least of all, those who in North America are called "born-again Christians." Of 100 people taken at random, 15 will be practicing Catholic Christians, eight will be Protestants, seven will profess another religion or none at all. Most probably, however, the other 70 will be baptized Catholic and will occasionally attend mass, weddings, funerals or special religious feasts. All of them have been shaped by the Christian ethos in its Catholic tradition.

Latin America is the only continent in the Third World with a Christian majority. It has the greatest Catholic concentration of the Christian West. Brazil is the biggest Catholic country in the world. (It is Brazil, as well, where two-thirds of Latin American Protestants live and where the biggest Spiritualist community can be found.) By the year 2000 Latin America will have *half* of the Catholic population of the world!

Christianity came to Latin America with the Spanish and Portuguese conquerors in the sixteenth century. Evangelization was

2

the spiritual side of the conquest, carried on by Franciscan and Dominican friars. Christ and the King, the cross and the sword came together. This was pre-Reformation Christianity—Iberian-style, fanatic, defensive, untouched by the new life of the Protestant Reformation. For the inhabitants of these lands Christianity was not a liberating gospel but the religion of domination. There were some outstanding exceptions, such as Father Antonio Montesinos and Friar Bartolomé de las Casas—the champions of the Indians—who represented a humanitarian trend of Christianity that has for centuries been latent. The church was an integral part of the colonizing and civilizing enterprise, transplanting the whole structural and ideological style of life of Catholic Christendom. The American Indians responded to this conquering and civilizing evangelization with passive resistance: adopting the whole package without really assimilating the Gospel. The result has been a pervasive syncretism of the masses or what is sometimes called a Christo-paganism. Christ was known as the Lord in Heaven, the Conqueror Christ (whose representatives on earth were the pope and the king), and as the Victim on the Cross. The submissive Indians could easily identify themselves with the martyr of Golgotha, the suffering and powerless Christ. Contemporary Catholic missiologists openly recognize that this kind of evangelization was in fact spiritual colonization.

Popular Religiosity

Catholic influence goes even deeper into the Latin American soul and culture. *Popular religiosity* is a widespread phenomenon which is the object of study and discussion in contemporary Latin America. This popular Catholicism includes vows and promises, pilgrimages and multiple devotions and the reception of the sacraments, particularly baptism and the first communion. Popular piety is strong on worship of the Virgin Mary (today boosted by Pope John Paul II's visit to Mexico and the Guadalupe Marian shrine), and the veneration of saints. Sanctuaries not only become centers of miraculous healing and divine answers to all kinds of prayers but tourist attractions selling images, candles and tokens. In this popular religiosity there is a resilient, simple faith in God, mixed with superstition and fatalism. But there are also important Christian virtues and moral values, relevant to family life, sexual behavior and a sense of celebration. These values also harbor double standards—*machismo* and permissiveness. This residual Christianity survives the secularizing impact of urban life and its mores, the powerful effect of the media and the deterioration produced by misery and promiscuity in the city slums.

Some radical Christians look at this popular religiosity as an alienation of the masses from reality and the struggle for social justice; other perceive in it social values and a potentiality for the people's liberation. Severino Croatto, Bible professor at Instituto Superior Evangélico de Educación Teológica (Ecumenical Theological Institute) in Buenos Aires, Argentina, makes a very critical assessment of popular religiosity from the perspective of the Gospel:

> The Church appears as the refuge of the oppressed masses, deepening their alienation, not offering them a critical [questioning] faith which can arouse their consciousness about their own situation of slavery. There are expressions of popular Catholicism which are the opposite to a liberating faith and which internalize oppression instead. The popular celebrations of death, pain and suffering, such as La Dolorosa,* the Holy Death, the Cross, are sort of ambiguous symbols. They help to accept with resignation suffering and oppression as the loving will of God, forgetting that they are caused by people.
>
> The tragedy is that this identification with the dying Christ has a great power of sublimation, introjecting in the people's conscience their situation of poverty and exploitation as an "imitation of Christ." But it is an imitation of his death—without resurrection. There is no expression of the resurrection in their economic and social lives. The oppressors are happy that the people celebrate Holy Week without resurrection. . . . The Christian, in identifying himself/herself with the dead and resurrected Christ, can look at his/her future of resurrection beyond this life, but also his/her anticipated resurrection in this life, looking towards new situations. This is why faith is subversive, demanding a change, the passing from death to life in every human order. Unfortunately, the resurrection has no such place in popular religiosity.[2]

Sometimes popular religiosity is considered an obstacle to evangelization, sometimes an asset. Anyway, it is a factor we have to reckon with in evangelization in Latin America today. The second Conference of Catholic Bishops of Latin America (CELAM), in its meeting in Medellín in 1968, recognized this fact, saying that in popular piety we can find "the secret presence of God," "the seeds of the Word," "an evangelical preparation," but that a "re-evangeliza-

---

*The seven stages between Christ's sentence and Calvary.

tion" and a "re-conversion" are necessary. "What we need"—some said—"is not to baptize the convert but to convert the baptized." The third CELAM Conference, in Puebla in 1979, also pointed to the positive and negative aspects of popular religiosity and called participants "to evangelize once again the religion of the people," appealing "to the Christian memory of our peoples."

We believe that this is something for us Protestants as well to ponder, as part of our own evangelistic strategy. What is "revival," after all, but "appealing to the Christian memory of our people"? And we wonder if the call of Puebla "to evangelize once again popular religiosity" might not also apply to our middle-class piety (another form of popular religiosity, a mixture of Gospel values and the bourgeois values of our society). In Latin America we have heard of what those in the United States call "civil religion" or "the American way of life." Could those forms of popular religiosity be evangelized?

Protestant Missions

Some of my neighbors in the South are Protestants.

Protestantism came to Latin America almost four centuries later than Catholicism—about a century ago. The introduction of Protestant Christianity was not easy, and it was fiercely resisted by the Roman Catholic Church until the Vatican II Council in the '60's. The forerunners of Protestant missions in Latin America were the colporteurs from the British Bible Society, who carried the Bible—unknown and prohibited—throughout the 20 Latin American republics. The Protestant version of the Gospel was strongly biblical, Christ-centered, ethical and individualistic, in contrast to traditional Catholicism with its Bible illiteracy, its popular veneration of Mary, its liturgical emphasis, and its hierarchical authoritarianism. Protestantism was considered an intrusion into a Christian land and rejected through legal pressure, social ostracism and even religious persecution. Some missionaries from North America saw this "invasion" as a crusade into the "Pope lands" of the South. But, for many of us, the Protestant missionary presence, and the churches that developed from it, represented the unique opportunity to have a personal experience with the living Christ, access to an open Bible, and the commitment to a life of freedom and moral seriousness. This testimony can be repeated all over Latin America by first-, second- and third-generation Protestant Christians.

Gradually and painfully the Protestant missions were able to get a modest foothold in this "officially" Christian territory, mostly among artisans and immigrants who were not so identified with the traditional and monolithic Latin American society. At the beginning of this century the Protestant community in all 20 republics totalled barely 50,000, fewer than one per 1,000 inhabitants.

There were those, however, who favored the introduction of Protestant Christianity in Latin America, particularly the new elite that was looking to the Protestant European countries and the United States for new models of "modernization." Latin American intellectuals and anti-clerical freemasons—who stressed freedom over against the backward Catholic clergy's dogmatism—looked to the Anglo-Saxon world as their model and to Protestantism (the religion of freedom and responsibility) as a timely ally against religious and political conservative forces. They were not interested in the Gospel as such but in the ideological and social implications of the Protestant presence. Second- or third-generation Protestants today, though grateful to the missionary work of the past and faithful to their Protestant faith, are looking more critically at the historical meaning of that presence and work. Some of them, like Dr. José Míguez-Bonino, are saying that as the Catholic evangelization was the spiritual side of Spanish or Portuguese "colonialism" in the sixteenth century, the work done by the Protestant missionary (willingly or unwillingly) was the spiritual accompaniment of the modernization project of "neo-colonialism" in the nineteenth century.[3]

When the Panama Congress on missions in Latin America took place in 1916, there were 10,000 Protestant members. Most of the delegates, however, represented the North American foreign missions working in the region; only 16 were Latin American delegates from the national churches. The mood was optimistic, and there was a strong conviction about the call to missionary work in Latin America. The strategy for the future was laid down, and its holistic methodology—evangelization, youth and women's work—was effective during the following 50 years. The spirit of cooperation among the mission boards was strong and the Cooperation Committee of Latin America was born, the first ecumenical institution to exist in this part of the world, the predecessor to the present Latin American Department of the National Council of Churches in the USA.

In the twentieth century new missions continued to come in. After the Second World War, when the missionary frontier in China was closed, Latin America became the center of interest for missionary activities, and a flood of missionaries came from North America. While the first missionary thrust came mostly from mainline mission boards, the bulk of the new missionary force came from the so-called "conservative" boards and "faith missions." The phenomenal increase of missionaries from North America in all the world (70 percent in the '70s) was also reflected in Latin America, where 32 percent of the North American missionary force were concentrated, totalling 11,000 Protestant missionaries. It is interesting to add that the same phenomenon took place in the Roman Catholic missionary work. While in the past most of the missionary priests, friars and nuns came from Spain and other European countries, in the '70s half of the 13,000 foreign priests in Latin America came from North America.

Church Growth in Latin America

The Protestant community has been growing steadily since 1930. By 1936 it had jumped to 2,400,000 members. While the population only grew three percent annually, the evangelical membership grew 10 percent, doubling itself every ten years.[4] In 1973 the Protestant community was estimated at 20 million members, somewhere between seven percent and eight percent of the total population. Two-thirds of them live in one country, Brazil. Two-thirds of the total are Pentecostals. Another interesting observation: these figures do not confirm the common assumption that the greater the number of missionaries from abroad, the greater the evangelistic work and church growth. For example, 750 or so missionaries from the NCC's related boards of mission, are working in churches representing 25 percent of the Protestant community, while 10,000 missionaries from "conservative evangelical" bodies are working in churches representing three percent of the total Protestant community. Meanwhile, the Pentecostals, who have very few missionaries or no missionaries at all from abroad, have the fastest growing churches on the continent. These facts show us that we cannot assess the importance and meaning of the missionary presence merely in terms of the number of missionaries or in terms of church growth figures.

The Pentecostals emerged at the beginning of this century and soon became the first indigenous Protestant movement in Latin America.[5] Chilean Pentecostalism sprouted from Pentecostal experiences within the Methodist Church, under the leadership of an American Methodist missionary, Willis C. Hoover. After their expulsion from the Annual Conference in 1909, the movement expanded to a membership of more than one million persons throughout its several different branches. The Assemblies of God in Brazil established congregations in every state, becoming the largest evangelical church in Latin America, with 1.5 million members. The Congregation of Brazil and Brazil for Christ (this last has the largest evangelical temple in the world, with a capacity of 24,000) grew mainly through the work of lay members.

This fantastic growth has intrigued sociologists, missiologists, church executives and experts from Christian and secular circles. Some give spiritual reasons, such as the free action of the Holy Spirit. Some find anthropological roots, i.e., people's hunger for God. Others offer sociological explanations: the Pentecostal community provides shelter, security, authority and identity for the rural migrants facing the anonymity of the big city. Still others find the answer in an appropriate pastoral methodology: lay participation, common people communicating the good news to common people in their own language and from their own situation. There are psychological and cultural explanations, such as the freedom of worship, the use of folklore music and instruments. The fact is that they are large, self-supporting, self-governed and self-multiplying churches, rooted among the poor masses, while the historical Protestant churches are confined to middle-class enclaves. Pentecostals do not lack problems of leadership, education, division and social alienation, but there is no doubt that they have a significant place in the future of Christianity in Latin America and a decisive role to play in the future of Latin American Protestantism.

"The cry of my people" is the cry of a Christian people, at different stages in their pilgrimage but sharing the common lot of the Latin American people.

Who Is My Neighbor? An American

My neighbor is an American.

This may sound strange to a citizen from Canada or the U.S.A. who is not accustomed to thinking of a Latin American as being American. There is a strange history behind the use of the word "American."

In fact, it has been called "a comedy of errors" by Germán Arciniegas, an illustrious Colombian writer. "The confusion over the name *America*," says the former professor of sociology at Columbia University in New York, "has no parallel in any other portion of the globe."[6]

The first act in "the comedy of errors" happened when the Spanish and Portuguese discoverers and conquerors of these lands called the native inhabitants *Indians*. They sailed to find a new road to India, and when they landed in La Hispaniola (today's Haiti and Dominican Republic), they thought they had touched Asia. The Spaniards and the British for four centuries spoke of the "West Indies." Christopher

Columbus died without knowing that he had discovered a new continent, believing he had reached Japan and that the Caribbean islands were a Japanese archipelago!

The second act in the "comedy" happened when the European cartographers named the New World *America*, honoring Amerigo Vespucci, the chief pilot of the Castilian monarchy who made four trips to the New World and who was the first one to realize that it was a new continent. So all those who were natives of this continent or descendants of the European migrants to these lands—whether in the northern, central or southern subcontinents—became *Americans*.

The third and most intriguing act of the "comedy" occurred when the 13 British colonies in North America won their independence, calling themselves the *United States of America*. According to Arciniegas, they did not have a proper name like the United States of Mexico or the United States of Venezuela or the United States of Brazil. Somehow, one part of America took on the name of the whole continent. George Stewart says that "the generic name of the United States was accepted as a provisional denomination after the search in Philadelphia for a suitable name to give the new republic had been postponed." Later on a plan was formulated to give the country the name of *Columbia* or *Colombia* in honor of Columbus. But Simon Bolivar had already adopted the name "Colombia," invented by the Venezuelan Miranda in 1806, for the old viceroyalty of New Granada in the South. Someone then suggested christening the country of freedom in the North *Freedonia*. But at that time a wag wrote a letter to a newspaper in the South pointing out that *donia (doña)* means *lady* in Spanish, and *free-donia* would mean *free ladies*! And that was the end of that. "As a consequence the United States is the only country in the world without an unmistakable name." And we, the citizens of other American countries, have to live with the fact that, in common parlance, to say *American* doesn't mean us but the citizens of the U.S.A.—one part of the American continent.

The final act of "the comedy of errors" is to call ourselves *Latin Americans*. What is so Latin about us? Yes, our lands were discovered and conquered by two Latin powers of the sixteenth century, Spain and Portugal. Another Latin country, France, later on had a foothold in Haiti and in French Guyana. Later on Italians came by the millions. But there were also important immigrant waves from Germany, Great Britain and other non-Latin European countries.

Sometimes the name is reduced to *Ibero-America*, referring to the two countries of the Iberian Peninsula, Spain and Portugal. But what about the "Indians," the original population of the hemisphere? So those who stress our native roots have proposed *Indo-America*. But then where do you place the European descendants, the African population, and the people of mixed races who are such a sizable proportion of the population and influence on the culture? *Latin America*, useful as it may be, is "at best, a tolerated misnomer."[7]

By this time we may be ready to acknowledge that there may be not one America but at least four Americas, about the same size, yet representing four historic zones, four experiences, four styles of life and four characters:

1—*Hispano-Indian America*, which is made up of 20 republics in South, Central and North America, covering 3,800,000 square miles
2—*Portuguese America* (Brazil), with 3,200,000 square miles
3—*English America* (United States of America), with 3,549,000 square miles, including Alaska
4—*Anglo-French America* (Canada), with 3,400,000 square miles.

The four Americas have a significant pre-Columbian history, with a great variety of Indian cultures which are pretty much alive today in North, Central and South America, with developed civilizations—a marvel to be admired by all generations—in what is called Meso America and the Andean region. But it was the different European and African contributions, geography and the historical experiences that made for new differentiating traits between our Americas.

Germán Arciniegas concludes, "To us these four Americas are four great provinces of a continental mass, moving along their separate paths in search of the same thing: freedom."

This is the main reason we need to know what we have in common and what separates us, if we are going to participate in a process of

awareness, identification and responsible action. "The cry of my people" is an American cry.

My Neighbor "Down There": The Third World

My neighbor is "down there."

It is common for the inhabitants in the northern hemisphere (or, for that matter, in the north of any country) to think of those in the South as "down there." Our maps and globes put the North in the upper part and the South in the lower part. Surely, it is just a convention, since in space there is no "above" or "below." Sometimes, however, this spatial location in our minds may have some subtle effects on our perspective of being "up" or "down."

There is a delightful comic strip character called Mafalda. She is an Argentine girl, six years old, always concerned with world affairs and speaking philosophically of serious adult things. One day she is with her friend Felipe looking at a big globe of the world. Felipe says, "I wonder why it is that all the poor countries are in the southern hemisphere, and all the rich countries are in the North?" Mafalda advances a theory: "It is because we are upside down, and all our good ideas fall off our heads!"

Those of us "down here" belong to what is called the *Third World*. This now common denomination has nothing to do with numbers, because it does not represent one-third of the world, as some may think, but two-thirds of the world in size and population.

Geographically, it is located mostly in the tropics and the southern hemispheres: Africa, Asia, Latin America, including the Caribbean and the Pacific Islands. Originally, Third World had an *ideological* connotation, applied to countries aligned neither with Western capitalism nor Eastern socialism.

11

Sociologically, the Third World has been described as marginal: the moving mass of humanity leaving behind its agrarian (rural) society without having access to the new industrialized society. The Third World, in this interpretation, is no man's land, an encounter between two civilizations, the world proletariat (working masses) of a global production system. It is formed by entire populations in movement, pushed out from their traditional means of life, becoming wanderers, without roots and without structures, looking for a future they don't know, and passing through the hardships and accumulated sufferings of this global mutation.[8]

Economically, the Third World has been described as "dependent" and "exploited." It is seen as an appendix of the world's industrial powers, assigned to be the producers of raw materials and the providers of cheap labor, exploited by the neo-colonialism of industrialized nations, transnational corporations and the financial centers of the world. The Third World is also controlled and exploited by the internal oligarchies and privileged groups in each individual country. For example, 30 percent of the world's population in the developed North consumes 85 percent of the earth's goods while 70 percent of the population in the underdeveloped South has access to 15 percent of the goods. The yearly per capita income* in the developed countries is U.S. $2,500 to U.S. $8,000; the yearly per capita income in the Third World is from U.S. $50 to U.S. $1,300.

World in Revolution

These facts about the "Third World" gave birth to the United Nations Conference on Trade and Development (UNCTAD), where the complaints, demands, and hopes for fair treatment and a New International Economic Order are aired by a group of 119 developing nations. The conflicts of interest with the industrial powers are obvious, particularly with the so-called Trilateral Commission, who represent the interests of the Big Three economic centers: Western Europe, Japan and the United States of America.† Seen from a Third World perspective, the real conflict in the near future is not so much between East and West but between North and South.

The Third World is a world in *revolution*. This is not a mere slogan. Latin America is going through a political revolution of the eighteenth century; the social revolution of the nineteenth century and the

---

*Division of the total national production by the number of people in the same country.

†See bibliography in Chapter Four.

cultural revolution of the twentieth century. All three at the same time!

In a sense, Mafalda was right: We in the Third World are upside down. We even feel good about it, because that is what the Gospel is all about—to put this world upside down. We are in good company. Paul and his companions disturbed the people in Thessalonica, who shouted, "These men have turned the rest of the world upside down, and now they are here disturbing the city!" (Acts 17:6)

Mafalda echoes the "cry of my people." A cry coming from the Third World, wanting to put the world upside down. This is not only a cry of anguish, of protest, of demand, but it is also a cry of hope, a cry of liberation. And we, as Christians, are called to join this cry in the name of the liberating Gospel of Jesus Christ.

How Many Neighbors? Population Growth

My neighbor is growing.

How many are my neighbors south of the Rio Grande? Let's first look at the people by country. The following table may help us:

TABLE I

Country	Area (Square Miles)	Population 1955	Population 1978	Per Square Mile
Argentina	1,078,769	19,300,000	26,395,000	24.5
Bolivia	416,040	3,190,000	5,285,000	12.7
Brazil	3,288,050	59,200,000	119,477,000	3.6
Chile	286,397	6,560,000	10,732,000	37.5
Colombia	439,520	12,700,000	25,614,000	58.3
Costa Rica	23,421	951,000	2,111,000	90.1
Cuba	44,206	6,110,000	9,718,000	219.8

Country	Area (Square Miles)	Population 1955	Population 1978	Per Square Mile
Dominican Republic	19,323	2,400,000	5,658,000	292.8
Ecuador	116,270	3,610,000	7,543,000	64.9
El Salvador	8,250	2,190,000	4,525,000	548.5
Guatemala	42,042	3,260,000	6,839,000	162.7
Haiti	10,714	3,300,000	5,534,000	516.5
Honduras	43,227	1,660,000	3,439,000	79.5
Mexico	760,373	29,700,000	65,421,000	86.0
Nicaragua	57,145	1,240,000	2,559,000	44.8
Panama	28,576	910,000	1,823,000	63.8
Paraguay	157,000	1,560,000	2,888,000	18.4
Peru	514,059	9,400,000	16,821,000	32.7
Uruguay	72,172	2,620,000	2,885,000	40.0
Venezuela	352,150	5,830,000	13,989,000	39.7

(Sources: United Nations, World Almanac, CELADE and CEPAL)

As can be seen by the third and fourth columns in the table, Latin America since 1955 has been growing fast. From 1800 to 1950, North America had the fastest growing population in the world primarily because of immigration. Latin America's population began to grow in 1900 and the growth has accelerated since 1950. It is now the fastest growing continent in the world, averaging three percent annually. It had 200 million people in 1950, is now reaching the 350 million mark, and is expected by the year 2000 to have 600 million people (9.4 percent of the world's population).

Young Population

This fact accounts for the phenomenon of a totally young population in the Latin American countries: more than 50 percent are under 19, 45 percent between 0-14 years old. Of course, this fact has tremendous implications for the economic and social prospects of Latin American countries, and also for the mission of the church! Population historically has been an asset for any nation or civilization, much more so in a region with such vast underpopulated areas. On the other hand, it creates tremendous pressures and demands on our societies struggling for development. "The cry of my people" becomes, in this statistical context, the cry of babies and children for adequate nutrition before they become deformed, damaged beyond remedy, or die. It is the cry of young people for education, the cry of new generations for jobs and meaningful participation in society, the cry of families for housing, food and health.

The explanation for this phenomenal growth is that, on one hand, we have an increase in birth rates while, on the other hand, we have a decrease in mortality rates, thanks to modern medicine, public health and better conditions of life. In most of our countries infant mortality is very high (every year 12 million children are born in Latin America and one million die).

There are, however, some other minor trends within this population explosion. Improvement in the standard of living and education brings down the population growth rates, decreases the birth rate, increases the senior population, and brings a stable middle-aged sector. Only four nations of the southern hemisphere have passed through this "demographic revolution": Argentina, Uruguay, Cuba and Chile. In the latter countries life expectancy is near 70 years, while in Haiti and Honduras it is 45 years. Among the Bolivian tin miners it has for a long time been 32 years, because of the inhuman working conditions in the "tunnels of death" which daily eat up their lungs with mine dust, producing tuberculosis and silicosis. The miners survive on a diet of little more than 1,200 calories a day.

This is one of the most stirring sounds coming from "the cry of my people." This is why many Latin Americans don't believe that the cry of growing, suffering and dying populations can be adequately responded to only by increasing the number of birth control programs. It is necessary also to provide more humane conditions of life for the millions of the South.

What Color Is My Neighbor? Races

My neighbor is multi-racial.

The Latin American population has been enriched with the blood strains of three continents.

Let's take the *Indians,* for instance, the original population of these lands. When the Conquistadores came in 1492 there were about 12 million Indians. At the time of Independence, around the 1820's, they had been reduced to eight million, decimated by epidemics (some of them imported from Europe) and by forced labor in the mines and ranches of the colonialists. In Peru alone, eight million Indians died in the mines during this period of three centuries. In 1825 the Indians began recovering their population, reaching 14 million in 1950 (nearer the original figure after four and one-half centuries), representing barely 8.8 percent of the total population. Today their number is around 30 million, still 8 percent of the total population.

The Indians have been able to survive better in the "central areas," where there are enough of them to live in communities keeping their own language, customs and community organization. Such is the case in the four "Indo-America countries"—Guatemala, Ecuador, Peru and Bolivia—where 91 percent of the Indians are concentrated, representing from 40 percent to 60 percent of the national population. Twenty percent of Mexico's people are Indian. There are also important Indian components in Colombia, Paraguay and some Central American countries. There are small Indian minorities in Chile, Brazil, Argentina and Venezuela.

The Indians' struggle today for survival is most acute among the small tribes located on the periphery of civilization, in the Amazon basin and tropical forests. They are running the risk of being exterminated by the "push" for progress, such as the mammoth projects of transnational corporations in Brazil or, in a more sophisticated way, through the "modernization" and "assimilation" projects of our governments.

"The cry of my people"—the Indians—is the cry for land, health, education, self-respect, self-determination and meaningful participation in the life of the larger society. This cry is beginning to be heard by churches who have not been totally alien to some refined ways of cultural annihilation. The church today is one of the few defenders of Indians' rights and integrity.*

The *blacks* (*negros* in Spanish) came to the southern hemisphere as part of what John Wesley called the "execrable villainy" of the slave trade from Africa. It was the sugar industry, first in the British Antilles and then in Brazil, that spurred the slave traffic from West Africa. It was, as well, a highly organized business that produced untold wealth for the sugar planters, the European merchants, the British traders, and the Latin American lords of coffee, indigo and tobacco plantations. Slavery was one of the major sources of capital during the first decades of the Industrial Revolution.

In Great Britain slavery was abolished because of the change in economic conditions and the impact of the anti-slavery movement, supported by the Methodist Revival and the spirit of the Enlightenment. But in Brazil slavery was not abolished legally until 1850, and it did not disappear in Cuba and Brazil until the last two decades of the nineteenth century. It is a sad comment on the missionary enterprise that some boards from the South of the United States chose Brazil as their field because slavery had not been abolished there.[9]

---

*See the *Declaration of Barbados*, sponsored by the World Council of Churches, the *Asuncion Document* produced by Latin American churches and missions, and the *Statement by the Catholic Bishops of the Amazonia, The Latin American Indian*, LADOC Series, Washington; USCC, © 1973. See also *The Indian in South America*, Geneva, WCC, 1972. See also *The Indian Awakening in Latin America*, Friendship Press, 1980.

In 1650 the black population was approximately 670,000. In 1825, after the independence period, it was 4.1 million (in that year alone nearly 2,000,000 slaves were brought into Brazil). In 1950 the black population all over Latin America was 13,729,111. This figure will be doubled by 1980, but over all blacks are a minority, trailing behind the Indians, with a bare six percent of the population.

Blacks, however, represent 90 percent in Haiti, 67 percent in the English–speaking Caribbean, 15 percent in Cuba, 13 percent in Brazil. A lower percentage is found in Colombia, the Dominican Republic, Ecuador, Venezuela and Puerto Rico. But their presence in music, dance, sports and religious movements goes far beyond their numerical size. African blood and culture are definitely integrated into the human and cultural streams of Latin America. Even white Brazilians can say with pride, "All of us have something of Africa in our souls."

So, in this "cry of my people," the blacks looking for a place in our societies are also a singing sound of freedom of the body and the spirit which is part of the African contribution to humanity.

The *white* populations have been growing steadily since the days of the Conquest. From 138,000 after the first century, to 4,349,000 at the time of Independence (around the 1820's) to 72 million in 1950, they were up to probably 150 million in 1978 (43 percent of the total population). The global figure of immigrants from Europe to Latin America was around 15 million between 1821-1932, mostly Spanish and Italians. The French, Belgians, Germans and Polish came in smaller numbers. European migration has stopped in the last decades, except for Venezuela, where 600,000 immigrants entered between 1950-1956.

Today the white populations make up 90 percent or more in Argentina, Uruguay and Costa Rica, 60 percent in Brazil, 50 percent in Chile, 37 percent in Venezuela and between 20-27 percent in the other countries, with the exception of Bolivia, where they are less than 15 percent. Even though whites are not the majority in all Latin American countries, they represent the dominant group, with the exception of Haiti and Paraguay. On the other hand, there are great masses of white people among the marginalized population, the oppressed lower classes and the impoverished low middle class of the "white zone" countries.* They join "the cry of my people" for a more humane and just society south of the Rio Grande.

The *Asiatic* component in Latin America is reduced to a few hundred thousand Japanese in southern Brazil, scattered Japanese

---

*Argentina, Chile, Uruguay.

colonies in Peru, Chile, Bolivia and Paraguay, and some Chinese colonies in Peru, Cuba and Panama.

Mestizos: The New Race

Mixed blood has been a distinctive feature of the Latin American human experience and a decisive factor in its population growth. The mixing of races began in the first years of the Conquest during the sixteenth century, producing the *mestizo* (Indian-white mixture). With the importation of a large number of slaves, the intermixture of European and African descendants gave birth to the *mulato*. Less common has been the mixture of Indian and black, the *zambo*, though such mixing took place in Brazil to a certain extent. (In Brazil people from this background are called *mamelucos*.)

The *mestizos* and *mulatos* together were 670,000 in 1650 (5 percent of the total population); 6.2 million in 1825 (27 percent of the population); 61.6 million in 1950 (38 percent of the population), and may be near to 140 million in 1980 (40 percent). People of mixed blood in Mexico make up more than 60 percent of the total population, about the same portion in Central America, Cuba, the Dominican Republic, Venezuela and Colombia. In Brazil they are close to 30 percent, while in Paraguay they go as high as 70 percent. In Chile they represent 50 percent of the total population.

This interracial product has played an important role in the molding of contemporary Latin America. In traditional society they were not accepted in the ruling white groups, but they felt themselves superior to the pure Indians and Negroes and distant from their European ancestors. It was among this group that nationalism found many of its most ardent adherents. They were artisans, clerks and gradually— through education—they have been able to play leading roles in several of our republics.

"The cry of my people" includes also the accents of this mixed race, searching for its identity and claiming its place as a truly American people, born of the clash of two cultures and the mixing in love of two bloods, the first fruit of the Old and New Worlds—the "cosmic race," as the Mexican writer Jose Vasconcelos has called it.

My Neighbor Inside the Structures

My neighbor is not an isolated individual. He/she belongs to a people, is part of a social class, is inside social and economic structures which set his/her limits and social probabilities.

First, we have the ruling group, the *upper class* or elite. In colonial times the upper elite was composed of peninsular* whites (later on replaced by *creoles*, their descendants); members of the Catholic hierarchy and owners of large plantations and export-import companies. Today the upper class is made up also of the urban industrialists and bankers, the high executives and technocrats, and top officers of the armed forces. As a rule, they constitute less than two percent of the people in any country. They control not only 65 to 80 percent of the cultivated land but also large-scale commerce and capital investments such as hotels, apartments and office buildings (increasingly through association with powerful transnational corporations). They have also been able to keep control of government and political life—openly or behind the scenes.

Then we have the always controversial and ill-defined *middle class*, or "middle sectors." In the past, they were made of small merchants and landholders; white collar workers, particularly in government service; craftsmen, and small industrialists. They were immigrants or children of immigrants or drawn from the upper or lower classes.

Through the increased role of the state in economics and social responsibilities, the expansion of the educational system, and the diversification of commercial activities, the lower stratum of these middle sectors has been increasing by the addition of bureaucrats, teachers, professionals, politicians, merchants, technicians, etc. John J. Johnson, professor of history at Stanford University, pointed to the emergence of the urban middle sectors as "one of the most profound developments" produced by industrialism and technological transformations. Based on the political influence of these middle sectors in five countries—Argentina, Uruguay, Chile, Costa Rica and Brazil—who favored industrialization, democracy, social legislation and moderation in politics, Johnson predicted that the middle sectors held the promise of the future for the Latin American republics. This assumption became an axiom for the Alliance for Progress in the '60s. The history of the last two decades has not confirmed those hopes and predictions.[11]

To begin with, numerically the middle class is still a minority. While in the United States the upper and middle classes together constitute about 80 percent of the population, in Chile they make up 21.4 percent; in Argentina 35.9 percent; in Venezuela 18 percent; in Mexico, 16.9 percent; in Brazil, about 15 percent; and in Guatemala, a meager 7.7 percent of the total population. In the majority of the countries they are less than 15 percent. Besides, their role in changing

---

*Spain and Portugal.

society has been ambivalent, dependent as they are on the upper classes and vulnerable to the inflationary process and economic deterioration. The middle-class mentality—identified with the values of the upper class—is afraid of social changes from below and tends to support the status quo. Others, however, become aware of their common lot with the lower classes. It is amazing to see that the radical thinking and participation in violent revolutionary movements came from the new generation among the middle sectors. Such was the case, for instance, with the urban guerrilla movement in Uruguay known as the Tupamaros, made up of well-educated young people from middle-class families.

At the Bottom

Finally, we have the *lower classes,* 80 percent of the population made up of workers, *campesinos** and marginalized people† of the city.

Workers have their unions to support them. In some cases, such as Argentina, the coordinated unions (2.5 million members) have had significant power in the country. But in the last decade even this right to associate themselves and participate in the economic and political life of the nation has been denied consistently in several countries.

Marginalized people are poor, illiterate and often jobless *peones*†† who look daily for pick-and-shovel jobs. Thousands arrive daily in the cities (rural migrants to São Paulo, Brazil, average 500,000 a year; a similar number arrive in Mexico City annually). In 1950, 25 percent (40 million) lived in cities; in 1975, 50 percent (150 million) lived in cities. The rural migrants to the cities have no steady work, do not belong to unions, sometimes do not know Spanish or Portuguese and frequently wear clothes typical of their rural communities.

A step below the urban worker is the small, illiterate white or mestizo farmer, living in the mountains, along the rivers, in a clearing of the jungle or isolated in the tall grass country, without schooling, without health care, and without a future. At the bottom of the scale are the *indigenous* people who speak no Spanish, do not know how to read or write, who cultivate their poor land as their ancestors did with oxen and a wooden plough, if they are fortunate or if not, a stick. When they are asked, "Why do you come to the big city?" their only response is, "It can't get any worse."

This is the cry of my neighbor. Shall I "recognize" him/her behind the facts and figures?

---

*Peasants.
†Term used in Latin America for large sectors of underemployed who live on outskirts of large industrialized cities.
††Rural workers.

2

NORTH AND SOUTH TOGETHER
For Better or For Worse

"For better or for worse," as we say in our marriage vows, Latin America and North America are bound together by geography, history, economics, geopolitics, and contemporary world issues. It goes without saying that Christian mission binds us together in an even deeper sense.

Mexico: The Next-Door Neighbor

Take, for example, the "special relationship" between Mexico and the United States. Both countries are bound together by geography: a common frontier, nearly 2,000 miles long, defined by the Rio Grande River, where "two worlds meet, blend and sometimes clash."

"Border Region Is Almost a Country Unto Itself, Neither Mexican Nor American" is the title of a fascinating article in the *New York Times,*[1] reporting on the development of the bicultural, bilingual cities spread all over this line "like the beads of a double-strand necklace," from San Diego and Tijuana in the west to Brownsville and Matamoros in the Gulf. The border is almost invisible and far from impenetrable. Fifty thousand legal commuters cross the bridges and official border posts daily, and thousands of Mexican workers cross the shoulder-deep stream illegally every day. Polluted air is carried by the wind both ways across the border. El Paso, Texas, cannot comply with the Federal air quality standards because of the polluted air that comes from Juarez on the other side. A lead smelter in El Paso, operated by the American Smelting and Refining Company, emits up to 75 pounds of lead-filled dust each day, and it is estimated that more than 8,000 children in Juarez, Mexico, between one and nine years old have abnormally high levels of lead in their bloodstreams. The Colorado River, which flows from north to south and on which many Mexican farmers depend to irrigate their fields, is becoming increasingly salty as more of it is drawn off by Americans to water their own crops.

In this particular symbiotic arrangement, the cities of the border region share their telephone service, currencies, food, language, clothing, architecture—and problems. The border, in fact, is a kind of magnet, attracting people by the millions from both heartlands. The traffic includes unemployed Mexicans from the rural areas (unemployment figures go as high as 50 percent of available manpower)[1]; Americans in search of bargains, buying French perfume, Mexican tiles or vine-ripened tomatoes at a nickel apiece; senior citizens and American families rushing southward toward the golden promise of the Sun Belt. Each year 82,000,000 people cross the border *legally,* that is 250,000 a day, 10,000 an hour. . . . Drugs used in the United States and contraband sought in Mexico also find their way across the border.

History has tied together and separated Mexico and the United States at the same time. The Southwest of the United States was colonized by Mexicans several decades before the Pilgrims arrived on the northeastern coast. Half of the original Mexican territory is now part of the United States.[2] When the Guadalupe-Hidalgo Treaty between the Union and Mexico was signed in 1848, two peoples with the same language and the same cultural heritage were left on both sides of the new line. On one side they remained "Mexicans"; on the other side they began to be called "Chicanos" or "Mexican-Americans," names used to this day, but they belong to the same people. The amazing development of that huge area of the Southwest was done by a combination of Anglo-Saxon adventurous creativity and determination on the one hand and, on the other, of Mexican manpower and knowledge of the economic activities of the region, such as mining, cattle raising, cotton harvesting, agriculture, and railway building. The land passed mostly to the Anglo citizens of the U.S.A., and most of the Mexican and Mexican Americans stayed as *peones* or seasonal workers.[3]

During the Second World War, the U.S.A. suffered from a labor shortage, and a first agreement was signed in 1942 for temporary employment of Mexican workers, "a *bracero* program"* which lasted 22 years. But in 1964, as a consequence of economic recession and unemployment after the Korean War, Operation Wetback was

---

Bracero comes from *brazo,* meaning *arm.*

mounted, producing mass deportations of more than one million Mexicans.

Other minor grievances, like the *Chamizal* controversy* and the exchange of prisoners, have been solved to both countries' satisfaction. But drug traffic, arms smuggling, contraband in antiquities, and illegal migrant workers are very touchy issues to be dealt with by these "uneasy neighbors" tied together by geography and history.

Pipeline Re-routed

Besides, the association of these next-door neighbors is mutually conditioned by *economy*. The United States is Mexico's first customer, taking 70 percent of its total exports and 85 percent of its present oil exports. And Mexico is the fourth customer of the United States and its sixth supplier of goods (not including the considerable border transactions). As for tourism to the United States, Mexico ranks only behind Canada. In 1975 Mexican visitors spent more than twice the amount spent by all European tourists. In the same year, income from investments, fees and royalties sent back to the United States totaled nearly $700 million. A good part of Mexican savings goes to American banks. No wonder, then, that Mexico's trade deficit with the United States went from $400 million in 1965 to $3.75 billion in 1975, and Mexico's external debt skyrocketed from $3.6 billion in 1971 to $20 billion in 1975. Ninety percent of this debt is with United States' private banks or with international lending agencies, with whom the United States exercises significant influence, such as the World Bank and the International Monetary Fund.

For the first time in its history, Mexico may now have the opportunity not only to balance its trade with the United States but also to spur its development. The discovery of large supplies of oil and gas in Mexico, in quantities rivaling the energy supplies of Saudi Arabia, has suddenly aroused the interest of the United States in its southern neighbor, and it has put Mexico into a new bargaining situation. The Mexicans want to go cautiously on this matter and to obtain lasting agreements, not just to react to opportunistic moves by

---

*This issue arose from the shifting course of the Rio Grande, raising the question of whether the Chamizal area was part of the Mexican town of Cuidad Juarez or of El Paso, Texas. In 1911 a Canadian arbiter ruled that two-thirds of the Chamizal was Mexican and only one-third belonged to the U.S. The U.S. refused to accept this judgment. (*US &LA: An Historical Analysis of Inter-American Relations,* Gordon Connell-Smith, Halsted Press, N.Y., 1974, p. 35).

its northern neighbor. This topic has been the subject of conversations between Presidents Jose Lopez Portillo and Jimmy Carter.

Professor E. J. Williams from the University of Arizona, an expert on oil, says that:

> In a gesture of friendship during the energy crisis of the hard winter of 1976-77, the Mexican government made a special point of offering oil and gas to the hard-pressed United States ("friends must help friends"). Indeed, by the early months of 1977, it appeared that the United States was receiving almost all of Mexico's petroleum exports—nigh to 150,000 barrels a day.[4]

Then came a clash with Energy Secretary James Schlesinger, just when an agreement to sell gas to the United States was ready, and a 900-mile pipeline from Mexico to the U.S.A. was under construction at a cost of $1.5 billion. Schlesinger vetoed the deal because he considered Mexico's price too high. The pipeline was re-routed to Monterrey, the northern industrial center. As President Carter learned in his visit to Mexico in 1979, Mexican pride was wounded. Presently negotiations were resumed and commissions appointed to deal with this issue and others between the two neighbor nations.

Illegal Aliens—"The Tortilla Fence"

One of those issues is the delicate "illegal alien" problem. Three million Mexican workers cross the border illegally every year, and one million of them are detected by the authorities. But some experts guess that about 10 million illegal Mexicans are living and working in the United States. They cross the border lured by the availability of work in the U.S.A. The millions of unemployed rural workers, even though they are not paid a fair salary (women are working for $1.00 a day, and men for $3.00-$4.00 a day), and even though they run the risk of being denounced and deported, keep on coming. As John Ehrlichman says "The economic forces that pull the Mexicans from their farms and villages are as irresistible as the law of gravity."[5]

The famous Nixon Number Two man, John Ehrlichman, became an unexpected witness to the problem of the so-called "Mexican aliens" after spending 18 months with Mexican prisoners in Safford Federal Prison in Arizona. His article deserves reading and to be circulated among Christians concerned with this problem. After living with hundreds of Mexican inmates and interviewing many of them, he has a lot to say about the recruiting system of Mexican workers, about the useless system of patrolling and detention, about discrimination against Mexicans in prisons, and about forced labor through police networks. He has something to say about the common complaint that "illegals" are a burden to the U.S.A. welfare program and an unfair competition for American workers, demonstrating with facts and figures that the Mexicans are doing the dirty jobs nobody wants to do, and that what they pay in tax revenues far exceeds the cost of the eventual service some of them get from welfare programs. He also points to the benefits the American employers get from Mexicans who work hard and work cheap. He ends with a surprising conclusion:

> We don't need electric fences and tough cops. If we are serious about cutting the illegals off, let Congress simply make their hiring a felony. Send a few employers to jail and the jobs will dry up.

> Such draconian devices would surely work, but we'd be poorer for it as a nation. The United States is enriched by the Mexicans who are here. . . . They are mostly good family folk who embody the work ethic. Sure, some of them are as

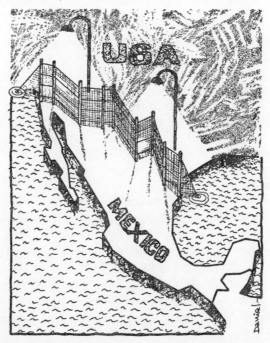

"The Tortilla Fence" by Daniel as taken from Migration Today,
Number 23, 1979, World Council of Churches.

unruly, dishonest, and immoral as some of their American neighbors. But most of them are quality people, as I learned from my eighteen months in the joint.

Here is a man who was at the top in the United States government and who fell down to the bottom, who had the opportunity to touch human life in its very nakedness, who heard "the cry of my people" of the border, and who raised his voice on their behalf. Our question then is, what are we going to do as Christians? What are Christians doing?

Mission—at the Doorstep

Surely, the problem of "illegal aliens" is a very complex and delicate one. The Mexican government and Mexican leaders are responsible for it and they will have to face it responsibly.[6] The U.S.A. authorities have their own responsibility, and they will be dealing with this issue in Congress. The American employers and workers and unions have their share in the problem and the solution. All Christian citizens have something to do as responsible citizens who look for human justice and the "peace of the city." But what is going to be the responsibility of our churches?

The Catholic Church has taken a clear stance on the matter. They have sided with the migrants, and they have raised the issue as a matter of human rights. Quoting Pope Paul VI in his 1969 "Instruction on the Pastoral Care of Migrants," they affirm that the human right to work and feed the family "precedes the right of a nation to establish borders and control exit and entrance to and from that nation."[7] El Paso Bishop Patrick Flores, after calling the Tortilla Fence "ridiculous, a foolishness," because "the hungry will break any barrier," declared that the best way to understand the undocumented was "by coming into contact with them, for the Word of God becomes incarnate when we become a part of other people." The Catholic Church has a network of 29 offices of Migration and Refugee Service.

What are the Protestant churches going to do in the United States? The same report quoted above says that United Church of Christ members, Episcopalians, Lutherans and Catholics have reached a consensus on the urgency "to do something for this human need; we must deal with human rights of persons, over and above the law." We have also heard of some churches providing special services for the undocumented migrants.*

---

*For example, Latin American United Methodist Church, 1350 Redondo Ave., Long Beach, Ca. 90804.

We are not the ones to say how the churches in North America can respond to this challenge. We cannot help but feel, however, that this is what mission is all about. Churches in North America have been very generous through the years in sending missionaries, funds, and prayers to the most remote areas of the world. But in this case of the migrant workers, mission is at your doorstep! The world is in the same place where the churches are, like the paralytic man at the doorstep of the temple (Acts 3).

What are we going to do? If we read the Bible with open eyes, we will discover that the Bible is the book of migrations and God is the God of migrants. Just think of the way God worked a purpose through the migration of Abraham's clan, "not knowing where he was going"; how God worked through Jacob's trip to Egypt, looking for bread in a time of hunger; how God used the selling of Joseph as a slave to the Egyptians; how God prepared his people through exodus, captivity, exile and return. . . . Christians are called in the New Testament "exiles and pilgrims" searching for a new city. . . . Migrants—legal or illegal—are not just problems. From a biblical perspective they are God's instrument to move history, they are—or they should be—for the church a missionary opportunity. If this is so, "the cry of my people" of the border should become the call from God.

The Panama Canal: The Jugular Vein of America

The Panama Canal, another common bond.

Panama is the jugular vein of America. It was written that geographically the Isthmus of Panama was going to be the continental and global land of contacts—or the land of contention. Simon Bolivar, who was a visionary as well as one of the great military geniuses of history, wrote in his Letter from Jamaica in September 6, 1815:

> This excellent position between the two great seas could become in time the emporium of the universe. Its channels will shorten the world distances, will tighten the commercial ties of Europe, America and Asia; they will bring to this so happy region the gifts from the four parts of the globe. Maybe, only there, one day the capital of the earth could be established, as Constantine pretended to do with Byzantium in the old hemisphere!

There were other dreamers as well. During the heyday of "Manifest Destiny" in 1890, when there was no longer any land frontier for the expanding nation of the north, Alfred Thayer Mahan of the Naval War

27

College at Newport, Rhode Island, wrote the famous book *The Influence of Sea Power Upon History*. The Caribbean Sea was the American Mediterranean for the author and, like the Mediterranean, it demanded a canal which would become not simply a prime commercial crossroads, but also a vital military highway. National greatness and commercial supremacy were related directly to supremacy at sea. The Panama Isthmus was the means to realizing that grandiose purpose.

Theodore Roosevelt was the first person of influence to read the book and grasp its importance. In his first message to Congress Roosevelt remarked that there was "no single great material work which remains to be undertaken on this continent of such consequence for the American people" as a canal in Central America. As David McCullough, whom we are following in these paragraphs, says in his best-seller, *The Path Between the Seas:*

> Roosevelt was promoting neither a commercial venture nor a universal utility. To him, first, last, and always, the canal was the vital—the indispensable—path to a global destiny for the United States of America. He had a vision of this country as the commanding power on two oceans, and these joined by a canal built, owned, operated, policed and fortified by his country. The canal was to be the first step to American supremacy at sea.[8]

But it was a Frenchman, the legendary Ferdinand de Lesseps, who built the Suez Canal, and a French company he organized, who started the gigantic venture of building a canal in the tropical Isthmus of Panama. When Lesseps was touring the U.S.A., promoting the canal enterprise, President Hayes sent a message to Congress clearly stating U.S. policy on the matter:

> An interoceanic canal . . . will be the great ocean thoroughfare between our Atlantic and our Pacific shores and *virtually a part of the coastline of the United States*. The policy of this country is a canal under American control.[9] (Italics added.)

The fact that the canal had to be built in *another* southern country didn't seem relevant. The U.S. President considered it "virtually part of the coastline" of *his* country.

The time came when the canal works could be bought from the French company, which was near bankruptcy. Theodore Roosevelt was the man called to lead this enterprise. But there was a complicated detail: the Isthmus of Panama belonged to Colombia, a South American country with which the United States had signed a treaty in 1846. In that treaty, the U.S. was granted "the exclusive right of transit across the Isthmus of Panama" and, in exchange, the U.S. granted "the perfect neutrality of the Isthmus" and Colombia's rights of sovereignty there. Colombia's government raised the matter of sovereignty and its participation in the financial deal in the canal treaty. After all, it was Colombian territory. But communications between Washington and Bogota were slow at the time and Washington decision-makers were eager to nail down the treaty. Pressure was exercised upon Colombia—including an ultimatum—indicating that the canal might be built in Nicaragua or that a separate treaty might be signed with the province of Panama. According to the press of the time, even "war with a South American Republic" was "being soberly contemplated."[10]

"Heterodox Arrangement"—"Remarkable Revolution"

President Roosevelt and his immediate collaborators wanted to act expediently. Their advisors had told them that "they were dealing with the slipperiest, most corrupt variety of Latin American and that the sovereignty issue was pure political hypocrisy." The President himself would speak angrily of "those bandits in Bogota," "those contemptible little creatures," and he warned that "we may have to give a lesson to those jack rabbits."

And expediently they acted. The fact that there was a long-held feeling for autonomy in Panama provided the necessary opportunity and instrument to get the thing done. Just a couple of days before the Panamanian delegates arrived in New York, the treaty was signed between the Secretary of State and Philippe Bunau-Varilla. Bunau-Varilla himself had a "ready-made revolution kit" for the Panamanian secessionists, including "a proclamation of independence, a basic military plan, a scheme of defense of Colon and Panama Cities, the draft of a constitution, a code by which he and the rebels could correspond." A modest loan was mysteriously processed to finance the revolution in Panama. Orders were given to the naval forces on the Pacific to sail toward the Isthmus. A secret mission was given to the commander of the warship *Nashville* to anchor at the Colon Harbor to prevent the landing of Colombian troops and to take control of the railway—the only means of communication that could be used by Colombian troops. A few days after the declaration of Panama's independence, 10 American gunboats arrived simultaneously at Colon on the Atlantic and at Panama City on the Pacific, in the best "big stick" style Roosevelt used to boast about. "I took the canal," he would say.

It was, concludes McCullough, "a heterodox arrangement" and "a remarkable revolution."

The American ambassador in Bogota, James T. Dubois, reminded his countrymen that "Colombian regard for the political ideals of the United States was enormous and that until 1903 Colombia was the best friend the U.S. had South of Rio Grande." Writing in 1912, nine years after the treaty, he added:

> By refusing to allow Colombia to uphold sovereign rights over a territory where she had held dominion for eighty years, the friendship of nearly a century disappeared, the indignation of every Colombian, and millions of other Latin Americans, was aroused and is still most intensely active. The confidence and trust in the justice and fairness of the United States, so long manifested, has completely vanished, and the maleficent influence of this condition is permeating public opinion in all Latin American countries, a condition which, if remedial measures are not invoked, will work inestimable harm throughout the Western Hemisphere.[11]

Those were realistic and prophetic words. "Remedial measures," in the canal issue, however, had to wait for more than 75 years. Meanwhile, this issue has been an inseparable component of North-South relationships—for better or for worse. Theodore Roosevelt would feel offended to be called an imperialist, but for "my people" who live in the "underside of history," *imperialism* would be a natural name for this kind of action.

The Panama Treaty

There were many American voices—universities, the liberal press—who protested against this "crime" and others who recognized that this was indeed a strange transaction. Senator Hernando de Soto Money (Miss.), conceded that the treaty:

> Comes to us more liberal in its concessions to us and giving us more than anybody in this Chamber ever dreamed of having . . . we have never had a concession so extraordinary in its character as this. In fact, it sounds very much as if we wrote it ourselves.

John Hay, Secretary of State, wrote to Senator Spooner:

> The treaty was very satisfactory, vastly advantageous to the
> U.S., and we must confess, with what face we can muster, not
> so advantageous to Panama . . . . You and I know too well
> how many points there are in this treaty to which a
> Panamanian patriot could object.[12]

Indeed. Panamanian patriots have been objecting for a long time
about the humiliating situation of a "colonial enclave" dividing their
nation in two by a 10-mile stretch—the Canal Zone.

The "patriot's objections" reached a crisis in 1964, when riots swept
the country and a group of Panamanian students, angered because
their flag was lowered by Zone students, marched into the Zone and
attempted to raise it but were repelled by fire from U.S. troops, who
killed some of them. This, fortunately, turned out to be the beginning
of more serious negotiations to review the treaty. They went on under
four U.S. administrations, culminating with President Carter's signing
the new treaty. The project is still under discussion by the U.S.
Congress at the time of this writing, and, if approved, it will become
effective in 2000, when the Canal and the Zone will pass into
Panamanian hands. Let's hope that this may be the beginning of a new
attitude and a new policy between North and South—for better, not
for worse.

In Latin America, the announcement of a new treaty has been
received with release and hope. Release from a sense of powerlessness
in the face of a long-lasting injustice and humiliating domination.
Hope that the treaty may become a first step in the right direction,
leading to an unconditional trusting of the canal in Panamanian hands,
the retreat from all military bases and the end of the training programs
for Latin American officers which have become the source of torturers
and repressers in Latin America during the last decade. In one word,
the hope of a total decolonization of Panama. General Torrijos, the
former President, has said, "Panama is engaged in an irreversible
process of decolonization." The Christian Congress for Peace, which
met in Panama City in April 1978, gave the Panamanian government
full endorsement of this aim and hope. The President, in his turn, had
already expressed his recognition that voices like the Christian
Congress for Peace "show to the world that the Christian word . . . is a
cry of hope for those who hunger and thirst for justice."*

---

*Primer Congreso Continental, No. 1, pp. 83–89f. See also New World Outlook
September 1975, p. 37; The Christian Century, Sept. 7, 1977, pp. 755f.; Jan. 1978, pp.

This cry for justice, is the *cantus firmus* of the "cry of my people"—in Panama and throughout all Latin America.

The Shadow of the Monroe Doctrine

Our relationships North and South, between the United States and all Latin American countries, have been, for more than a century and a half, under the shadow of the Monroe Doctrine.[13] This foreign policy guideline for the hemisphere was born in 1823, when the Latin American countries were at the peak of their struggle for independence from Spain. President James Monroe's message to Congress on December 2, 1823, said:

> We owe it, therefore to candor, and to the amicable relations existing between the United States and those (European) powers, to declare that we should consider any attempt on their part to extend their system to any portion of this hemisphere as dangerous to our peace and safety.

This was, as Secretary of State John Quincy Adams wanted it to be, a purely American statement of policy, a unilateral doctrine. The new nation was telling the European powers to keep hands off former European colonies in the southern hemisphere. The reason? Because they were part of the United States' security zone. This doctrine, in fact, supported the cause of independence of the new Latin American countries. But at the same time it meant that the new nations were born inside the self-declared hegemony of the northern republic. Here lies one of the oldest roots of problems for our relationships as new nations in the hemisphere. It is only fair to recognize that, after a hesitation of seven years, the United States became "the champion of the brave efforts of the other American nations to win freedom from Spain, France and Portugal," and it was the first outside nation to recognize the new Latin American states. That was a great service. And it was the origin of sympathy, admiration and prestige for the United States in the South.

But soon, confusing signals came in the application of the Monroe Doctrine. The Liberator, Simon Bolivar himself, was warned by John Quincy Adams against any attempt to free Cuba and Puerto Rico from Spanish rule. Besides, the U.S. kept silence in the face of British

13-18; April 1978, p. 347; *Latin America Press,* Lima, Peru, July 5, 1979; *Time,* October 31, 1977, p. 26; *Dallas Times Herald,* Nov. 20, 1977, p. G-3.

occupation of Honduras and the Falkland Islands (still a burning issue between Great Britain and Argentina, where the islands are known as the Malvinas). President Polk revived the Monroe Doctrine in 1845, when it seemed that European powers might try to prevent the United States' annexation of Texas from Mexico.

When in 1895 the United States claimed its right to arbitrate between Venezuela and Great Britain on the controversy over the Venezuelan-Guianan boundary, the implications of the Doctrine became clearer. Secretary Olney told the British, "Today the United States is *practically sovereign* on this continent and its fiat is law upon the subjects to which it confines its interposition."[14] (Italics added.)

Sad Story of Interventions

Then began a sad story of interventions by the U.S. in the life of Latin American nations. In 1897 the United States helped to prevent a Central American Federation. In 1898, the accidental explosion of the *Maine* in the Havana harbor led to the "splendid little war" against Spain that ended with the acquisition of Puerto Rico as a U.S. possession and effective control of Cuba, including the Guantanamo base in perpetuity. Cubans were obliged to accept the Platt Amendment that gave the U.S. the right to intervene in Cuba whenever, in the opinion of the American government life and property were threatened. Actually, the U.S. intervened in Cuba until 1934 and kept virtual control of the economy of Cuba until Fidel Castro came along in 1959.

President Theodore Roosevelt gave the Monroe Doctrine another twist, and it became openly interventionist with his famous *Corollary* of 1904:

> Chronic wrongdoing or an impotence which results in the general loosening of the ties of civilized society, may in America, as elsewhere, ultimately require intervention by some civilized nation, and in the Western Hemisphere the adherence of the United States to the Monroe Doctrine may force the United States, however reluctantly, in flagrant cases of such wrongdoing or impotence, to the exercise of an international police power.[15]

The U.S. was no longer a champion of freedom or a friend but a tutor, a self-appointed "police power." From now on, and for 30 years, interventions would take place at an average of two a year, not because of external powers intervening in America but because of internal conditions considered by the U.S. as "wrongdoing" or "impotence." In Haiti the occupation lasted for 19 years, in Nicaragua for 20 years, and in the Dominican Republic for eight years. In every case the U.S. Marines would help to establish "some of the nastiest, longest-lasting, and generally most vicious dictatorships that Latin America has ever seen."

The most pathetic case is President Wilson's interventions in Latin America. Wilson was one of the most admired statesmen in Latin America because of his idealism, his prestige as the founder of the League of Nations, his peace initiatives and his moral stature. He was a noninterventionist but he encouraged interventions in Mexico, the Dominican Republic and Haiti! Herbert L. Matthews of the *New York Times* says:

> The activities of President Wilson from 1913 to 1917 were the most blatant, inexcusable and futile examples of interventionism in the history of our relations with Latin America.[16]

What we learn from his experience is that to reach justice in international relationships, the good intentions of some statesmen are not enough. There are other factors involved, such as international structures, national policies, political pressures, economic interests, military gravitation, and so on. It helps us to understand that *imperialism* is not reduced to territorial conquest (Wilson had said, "The United States will never again seek one additional foot of territory by conquest") but has to do as well with military interventionism, economic expansion, political control, or so-called "police power."

In 1926, the Marines were again in Nicaragua, this time to bolster U.S.-supported President Chamorro and to contribute in the hunt of the revolutionary leader Augusto Sandino, who was finally killed in an ambush by the Somoza clan. After the occupation, the Marines turned the country over to a Marine-trained officer named Anastasio Somoza. The Somoza dynasty ruled the country with an iron hand for 46 years. In 1979 after all those long years of repression and suffering, 30,000 dead, material destruction by Somoza's bombings and atrocities committed by his National Guard, the Nicaraguan people, led by the Sandinista army, have started a new period of national reconstruction. This time the U.S. played a low-profile role. Initially the U.S. attempted a collective intervention by the Organization of American States, which was strongly resisted by the Andean countries and Mexico. In withdrawing its military support to Somoza, the

U.S.A. helped in the final breakdown of the tyrant's regime. Latin American countries recovered their own dignity by sticking to their own decisions, and U.S. foreign policy showed signs of the old Good Neighbor Policy.

The Good Neighbor Policy

During the Depression years, the Monroe Doctrine, as it has been interpreted and enforced, began to decline and interventionism faded away. In 1928, Secretary J. Reuben Clark criticized as "unjustified" Theodore Roosevelt's Corollary. In his inaugural message in March 1933 the new President, Franklin Delano Roosevelt, formulated what was going to become a historic new policy:

> I would dedicate this nation to the policy of the Good Neighbor—the neighbor who resolutely respects himself and, because he does so, respects the rights of the others.

That same year, the Panamerican Conference in Montevideo affirmed the principle of "non-intervention in the internal affairs of other states." Cordell Hull signed the Declaration on behalf of the United States. The following year the Platt Amendment was abrogated and the Marines were withdrawn from Haiti and Nicaragua. When President Lazaro Cardenas of Mexico nationalized the American oil companies, there was no American intervention. Those were the years of the Good Neighbor Policy. And for this FDR will always be remembered in Latin America, and his Good Neighbor Policy will always be a point of reference in our relationship North and South.

During the Second World War, the Good Neighbor Policy paid off well. With only Chile and Argentina hesitating, all Latin American countries moved from a "benevolent neutrality" towards active support of the Allies' cause, declaring war on the Axis and, as proper allies, supplying raw and strategic materials at reduced prices. Nazism was a real threat, and all sympathies were with the heroic Great Britain and the United States' participation in the war. The Monroe Doctrine was expressed in those years with the slogan: "America for the Americans."

Cold War Anti-Communism

Then came the years of the Cold War. The United States had become the world champion against "international communism."

"The right to live" by Solón.

Foreign policy was determined by "rabid anti-communism": any government was supported, no matter how dictatorial and repressive, provided it professed anti-communism. And any government would be sabotaged or directly overthrown if suspected of leftist leanings or engaged in social reforms that might affect the interests of foreign capitalistic enterprises. This time, however, a collective instrument had been created for intervention and the implementation of the old Monroe Doctrine, which was altered again and again by the Truman-Acheson and Eisenhower-Dulles administrations. In 1947 the Rio de Janeiro Pact of Reciprocal Assistance was signed, and in 1948 the Organization of the American States (O.A.S.) was created. In 1954, in the Caracas Conference of the O.A.S., Secretary John Foster Dulles was the architect of the resolution which was, in fact, the new version of the Monroe Doctrine:

> The domination or control of the government of whatever American country by a communist movement constitutes a threat to the peace and sovereignty of all republics.

Seven of the worst dictators of Latin America signed this "democratic" declaration. This was the preparation for the condemnation of the Guatemalan regime, involved in some moderate social and economic reforms that might affect the interests of the United Fruit Company, which had the monopoly on ports, railways and agricultural exports. In a short time a small army trained and financed by the CIA entered from Nicaragua and took over the Guatemalan government.

Crisis in the Inter-American System

In 1965 a democratic movement was regaining control in the Dominican Republic. This time 20,000 Marines invaded the country, once again without any collective action by the O.A.S. This was the "coup de grace" for Latin American consciousness of the real value of the inter-American system. Power was power, and it was the decisive factor, no matter how good the judicial construction of the Organization of American States might be, or the reiterated declarations about "non-intervention in the internal affairs of the states." The strong and negative reactions received by Vice President Nixon in his Latin American tour of 1958 have to be seen in the context of the recurring American interventions in Latin America.

The most critical point by far in hemispheric relations was the Cuban

Revolution. The United States' reaction to a socialist regime in Latin America was a blunt rejection. It led to the cutting of the sugar quota (a survival issue for the Cuban economy), a boycott and blockade, the expulsion of Cuba from the O.A.S. because of U.S. pressure, the invasion of the Bay of Pigs, and—as is now known from CIA revelations—the attempt to assassinate Premier Fidel Castro. The Latin American states broke ties with Cuba, some (mostly dictatorships) gladly, others (some of the democratic regimes) reluctantly. Only one, Mexico, kept its autonomy, deciding to continue formal diplomatic relationships with the new Cuban regime.

When the missile crisis involving the United States and Russia occurred, the spontaneous response of Latin American countries was unanimous support for the United States. This time it was a matter of life and death, of peace and war in the hemisphere, not a matter of ideological warfare against the internal politics of another country. So the usual manipulative tactics behind the scenes were not necessary. The Monroe Doctrine probably made more sense in this context, one of confrontation in our continent between the two great world powers.

According to Celso Furtado, a noted Brazilian economist, the Cuban missile crisis was an attempt to bring the Monroe Doctrine up to date:

> According to the new rules, two options are open to the countries in Latin America: political and economic integration under U.S. hegemony, each particular situation being defined within the sphere of influence of the superpower, or dislocation from the sphere of influence. In the latter event, however, the country in question can only hope to have its sovereignty "tolerated" according to the rules laid down for each individual case by the dominant power.[17]

A Satellite Area?

This may explain—however paranoiac it may sound to our U.S. friends—why so many Latin Americans feel that we belong to a sort of satellite area. Of course, we have freedoms and possibilities that are not evident in the Soviet Union satellites, but, on the other hand, there are specific limits to our nations' self-determination, and we are far from a relationship "between equals." This fact is essential for understanding and accepting our relationships North and South—for better or for worse.

The Alliance for Progress, launched by President Kennedy and continued under President Johnson—no matter what its economic results—was an attempt to revive the Good Neighbor Policy with a constructive effort for economic development and social reform. During the Nixon years the Alliance receded and the model of "association" in the hemisphere took the form of growing private enterprise operations and continuing and enlarging military aid and assistance to armies and police forces—which became very effective for repression in this decade of captivity. Many other ways of cooperation which had begun in former years have continued during this decade.

Today President Carter's publicized campaign for human rights, the new Panama Canal treaty, respect for the Nicaraguan revolution, and the apparent openings to Cuba may well be hopeful signs. Credibility needs to be established. The Good Neighbor Policy existed during 15 years of our 155 years of independent life as nations and mutual relations with the U.S. Maybe it's time to try again, for we are bound together—for better or for worse.

"The cry of my people" is a cry for dignity and mutual respect, North and South. It is a cry for better, not for worse.

3

THE MIRAGE OF ECONOMIC GROWTH
The Development of Underdevelopment

Those who have a superficial acquaintance with Latin America easily associate it with the words like *mañana* (tomorrow) and *siesta* (nap). A common stereotype for the inhabitant south of the Rio Grande is a Mexican sleeping under a big hat. It is also a common illusion for the more fortunate to think that they "have" because they work hard, and the poor "have not" because they are lazy. Of course, these are caricatures, like those representing a North American as a cowboy or as a Wall Street tycoon with a top hat, tuxedo, striped trousers, pockets filled with dollars and smoking a big cigar!

It would be much simpler to explain away the problem of underdevelopment as a matter of Latin laziness. The seeming "laziness" of poor people is very often nothing else than the lack of sufficient vitamins and proteins in their diet. But the plantation workers in Central America cutting sugar cane from sunrise to sunset do not work less than the executive in his plane or in his modern office suite or the secretary at her desk working eight hours—with coffee and lunch breaks—five days a week. The Indian farmers of the highlands enjoy no Sundays, for it is market day for their products. The urban dwellers of Mexico City, Buenos Aires or São Paulo don't even remember the *siesta*—unfortunately!

No, Latin America has not been sleeping *siestas*. South American people have been working hard—with the exception of those forced into unemployment. Workers in southern factories are able to use new machines as well as their counterparts in the North. Latin American technocrats have been quick to learn, to project, to organize and to increase productivity. It certainly is not lack of hard work that causes "underdevelopment."

Economic Growth—Not Human Development

During the last decade Latin American gross national product (GNP) has been growing steadily. Indeed, the southern hemisphere has been one of the most dynamic areas in the world in economic growth and productivity. In 1950, the GNP was worth $60 billion; it was $220 billion in 1974, and $334 billion in 1977. During the early '60s, the real growth rate (with inflation removed) was 7.6 percent annually. It slowed down during 1977, a recession year, to a 4.5 percent annual increase (the annual increase of developed countries the same year was 3.7 percent). All in all, the average for the 1968-1978 decade was 5.8 percent annual GNP increase.

And yet, "underdevelopment" is here to stay, and "development" may be even further away on the horizon. . . . The lot of poor people has not improved. In fact, this decade has been harder for increasing millions in Latin America. The gap between the poor and the rich inside our countries has increased and the gap between the poor nations and the rich nations is even wider. Why? Because the gross national product grew but not the per capita income (PCI) of the vast majority of the working people. It is one thing to increase the national product and quite another thing to achieve a fair distribution of this increase among all members of society. Let's learn the name of the game: GNP is one thing, and PCI is another!

The "per capita income" (the GNP divided by the total population) was, in 1975, as follows.

Argentina	$1,301 a year	Nicaragua	$438 a year
Venezuela	$1,235 a year	Guatemala	$462 a year
Panama	$ 978 a year	El Salvador	$420 a year
Mexico	$ 967 a year	Ecuador	$415 a year
Uruguay	$ 880 a year	Dominican Rep.	$434 a year
Chile	$ 779 a year	Paraguay	$390 a year
Costa Rica	$ 728 a year	Bolivia	$276 a year
Brazil	$ 568 a year	Haiti	$105 a year
Colombia	$ 565 a year		
Peru	$ 564 a year		

(In the same year the United States PCI was $4,838 and the Canada Personal Disposable per capita was $4,520.)

The chart shows that in the countries in the right column, the majority of the people live at mere survival level. We have to realize that the PCI is an average figure, so that some people have a real income superior to those figures while that of others is much lower than the average. Taking Latin America as a whole, the upper 20 percent receives 66 percent of the total income, while the lower 20 percent receives only three percent of the total income. One-fourth of the total population in Latin America has a PCI less than $75.00 a year. During the '60s the per capita income was increased by one hundred dollars, but of that amount only $2 per capita reached the poorest 20 percent of the population. The Alliance for Progress had a very modest goal: to increase the PCI by at least 2.6 percent. It never happened—during the '60s or the '70s.

Spare Us This Development

One-third of the population is marginal to the whole process of productivity and industrialization: 100 million Latin Americans live under the extreme poverty line—undernourished, without health care or any education, crowded in one-room shacks, unemployed or under-employed, without access to the material and cultural goods of our society.

A decade ago, when Gary McEoin was doing a survey in Latin America for one of his books, he talked with Joel Gajardo, a young Latin American Protestant leader and a doctor in social and political sciences who worked in close touch with the poor in Chile (today he is the National Council of Churches director of the office on South America). Referring to the so-called "second decade of development," the '60s, Gajardo said:

> If this is what one decade of development does for us, spare us from another. The 1960s were the most disastrous decade in the entire history of Latin America. Instead of narrowing the gap between rich and poor countries, it grew significantly wider. Foreign aid from governments has been used, not to develop us, but to achieve the political purposes of the donors. Repayments of principal and interest will soon exceed new loans, if they don't already do so. In another ten years the mountain of debt will smother us. [This was a terribly certain prophecy, as we shall see.] As for foreign private investment, the impact is even more negative. The proportion of the working population employed in manufacturing has remained practically stationary at under 15 percent for forty years. Foreign firms are more interested in buying out local competitors than in building new factories. Profits and royalties exported far exceed the importation of new

capital. We no longer have a voice in our most basic decisions.[1]

What has been happening is the "development of underdevelopment," as it has been called by the economist André G. Frank. Development is not a stage that comes after underdevelopment—underdevelopment is a by-product of development! Both are inseparable, like the two sides of the same coin. This phenomenon has been explained also by Raúl Prebisch—a world-famous Argentinian economist who was for many years the head of the Economic Commission for Latin America of the United Nations—as the natural result of patterned relationships between the economic "centers" and the "periphery," a sort of "neo-colonialism." Some Latin American economists and sociologists have been analysing the whole situation in terms of the "Theory of Dependence," which is beginning to make inroads among the academic community of Latin scholars in the United States as well.[2]

The "dependence model" is as old as colonialism.

The Open Veins of Latin America

A Uruguayan author, Eduardo Galeano, has described the economic history of Latin America with the suggestive title *Open Veins of Latin America: Five Centuries of Pillage of a Continent*. He says:

Latin America is the region of the open veins. Everything, from the discovery until our times, has always been transmuted into European—or later United States—capital, and as such has accumulated in distant centers of power. Everything: the soil, its fruits and its mineral-rich depths, the people and their capacity to work and to consume, natural resources and human resources. Production methods and class structures have been successively determined from outside for each area meshing it into the universal gearbox of capitalism. To each area has been assigned a function, always in benefit of the foreign metropolis of the moment, and the endless chain of dependency has been endlessly extended. The chain has many more than two links. In Latin America, it also includes the oppression of small countries by their larger neighbors and, within each country's frontiers, the exploitation of big cities and ports of their internal sources of food and labor.[3]

43

In the last two sentences, Galeano has summarized what can be called the story of *colonialism, neo-colonialism,* and *internal colonialism!*

First, it was the *gold* from Peru and the *silver* from Potosí, Bolivia, and Zacatecas, Mexico, that flooded like water into Spain. Between 1503 and 1660 no less than 185,000 kilograms of gold and 16,000,000 kilograms of silver arrived at the Spanish port of Sanlúcar de Barrameda. The silver shipped to Spain in a century and a half exceeded three times the total European reserves. But while "Spain owned the cow, others drank the milk": most of those riches were siphoned to German, Genoese and Flemish bankers—the cradle of modern capitalism. Meanwhile Latin America held the skeletons of millions of Indians sacrificed in the mines, the memories of the passing splendors of the city of Potosí, and kilometers of tunnels and holes in the hills.

In 1703 gold began to flow from the famous mines of Ouro Preto (Black Gold), Brazil, going out to the Portuguese metropolis, where it was transferred to England in exchange for wine, manufactured products and African slaves. In the eighteenth century, Brazilian gold production exceeded the total volume of gold that Spain had taken from its colonies in the two previous centuries. Holland and England—the leading gold and slave contrabandists—amassed fortunes in the illegal "black meat" traffic. Brazilian gold was channeled to London by licit as well as illicit methods. According to British sources, the value of gold reaching London was £50,000 a week. Meanwhile, there remained in Brazil only the big churches, the works of art and millions of slaves brought from Africa. Slaves died after a few years of forced labor, but "the Portuguese were meticulous in baptizing them all before they crossed the Atlantic. . . ."

The "cry of my people" has a long history and it is transcontinental. . . .

Bitter Sugar

Then came the *sugar* cycle, to satisfy the demand of the European markets and the hunger for riches of merchants from the Netherlands, France, England, and, later on, from the United States. The whole Northeast of Brazil was mushrooming with sugar mills and the "sugar islands" of the Caribbean became a more important asset for Great Britain than the 13 colonies of North America. To this day, Barbados, the Leewards, Trinidad-Tobago, Guadeloupe, Puerto Rico, Cuba, Haiti and Santo Domingo have been condemned to monoculture. The big plantation—worked by slave labor—became the antecedent of present *latifundio* (big rural estates) oriented towards the world market and subject to its caprices. While it spurred, directly or indirectly but decisively, the growth of the European centers, it left behind a "subculture of poverty, subsistence economy and lethargy." The same happened with the other agricultural "developments" in Latin America. Let Galeano summarize the story:

> The Northeast was Brazil's richest area and is now its poorest
> . . . In Barbados and Haiti, human antheaps lived condemned to penury; in Cuba *sugar* became the master key for the United States domination, at the price of monoculture and the relentless impoverishment of the soil. And this has not been the role of sugar alone; the story has been the same with *cacao*, which made the fortunes of the Caracas oligarchy; with the spectacular rise and fall of *cotton* in Maranhao; with the Amazon *rubber* plantations, which became the cemeteries of Northeastern workers recruited for a few pennies; with the devastated *quebracho* forests in northern Argentina and Paraguay; with Yucatan's *henequen** plantations, where Yaqui Indians were sent to extermination. It is also the story of *coffee*, which advances leaving deserts behind it, and of the *fruit* plantations in Brazil, Colombia and Ecuador, and the unhappy lands of Central America (the "bananization" of countries under the omnipotent United Fruit Corporation). Each product has come to embody the fate of countries, regions, peoples; and *mineral*-producing communities have, of course, traveled the same melancholy road. The more a product is desired by the world market, the greater the misery it brings to the Latin American people whose sacrifice creates it.[4] (Italics added.)

A similar story can be told about the tin mines in Bolivia, petroleum in several other countries, iron, manganese and strategic minerals in Brazil. In the huge area of the Amazonia, Brazil, photographed and mapped by the U.S. Air Force, which passed all the information to private investors, great extensions larger than Connecticut, Rhode Island, Delaware, Massachusetts and New Hampshire put together have been sold at the ridiculous price of seven cents an acre. General Riograndino Kruel, Federal Police Chief, told the Congressional investigating commission of Brazil that "contraband in materials containing thorium and uranium amounts to an astronomical one

---

*Sisal hemp.

million tons." U.S. citizens, accused of smuggling Brazilian atomic minerals, mysteriously fled the country. But smuggling is not always necessary. Legal concessions keep up the process of stripping Latin America of its resources.

All of us have been protesting about the increase in the price of coffee, but let's see where the increase really goes, according to the same author:

> It is much more profitable to consume coffee than to produce it. In the United States and Europe coffee creates income and jobs and mobilizes substantial capital; in Latin America it pays hunger wages and sharpens economic deformation. It provides work for more than 600,000 people in the United States: those who distribute and sell Latin American coffee there earn infinitely more than the Brazilians, Colombians, Guatemalans, Salvadoreans, and Haitians who plant and harvest it on the plantations. And, incredible as it seems, coffee—so ECLA tells us—puts more wealth into Europeans' state coffers than it leaves in the hands of the producing countries. In effect, in 1960 and 1961 the total taxes levied on Latin American coffee by European Economic Community countries amounted to about $700 million, while supplier countries got $600 million.[5]

"In the Mines" by Solōn.

The bleeding of Latin America illustrates how true it is that development produces underdevelopment; one goes with the other: development of the centers goes with underdevelopment of the peripheries.

The Tricks of Industrialization

Since the 1930s, Latin American countries have been trying to industrialize. World War II obliged the traditional industrial centers to concentrate on the war effort, a fact which provided the Latin American countries with the opportunity to develop national industry for the immediate needs of the internal market (food processing and textile industries, for instance). This industrialization of "import substitution" helped salaries and social benefits for the work force of the cities and for some countries it was possible to nationalize public services such as railways and electric plants.

During the last two decades or so, industrialization of the Latin American countries has aimed at processing some of the natural resources (wool, meat, leather, tin, oil, etc.) and producing them for exportation. Some countries, notably Brazil, Argentina and Mexico, have begun new industries, such as the "white line" (refrigerators, home appliances) and automobile production.

It was then that the "tricks" of industrialization started to become visible:

1) exports of manufactured products (or semi-processed raw material) depended on the opening of traditional markets—buyers of raw material—and they were exposed to protectionist measures from the traditional manufacturing centers;

2) to start new industries, technology and equipment had to be imported, and at a very high price;

3) loans had to be secured from outside investors, often with strings attached;

4) investment laws had to be changed and social conditions had to be created (or enforced by repression) to get stability, to avoid strikes, to insure high profit and quick investment return;

5) profits had to be exported;

6) licenses, fees and royalties had to be paid;

7) loans and interests had to be repaid in foreign currency and at adjustable rates;

8) production had to be oriented not toward the priorities of the majority of the population but toward the demands of the outside market or the "needs" of the minority where income was concentrated;

9) those who had control of the money and technology would not permit national industrialization, except in association with, or by selling out to, the transnational corporations.

So while increasing productivity, initiating industrialization and expanding exports, the rules of the game were such that the more the Latin American countries produced and exported, the more they became dependent and the deeper they got into external debt. These are the paradoxes or the contradictions of the "development of underdevelopment." They are as true today for industrialization as they were yesterday for export agriculture.

Here we see the mirage of economic growth without changing global or national structures—economic growth without human development.

This is so difficult to believe or to understand that it might help us to look at two specific examples of outward-oriented development and quick dependent industrialization: the tiny island of Puerto Rico and the huge land of Brazil.

Puerto Rico: A Showcase

The Puerto Rican experience may well be a showcase for the "development of underdevelopment," dependent development or outward-oriented development.[6]

Capital investments in Puerto Rico have passed through three different stages in this century, conditioning the life of the country, where the dominant factor has been the investor's profit and not Puerto Rican needs or interests.

During the first 50 years of this century, in the *first* "development" stage, investment was primarily in agriculture—sugar cane, tobacco—and some in manufacturing. Sugar cane occupied between 50 and 75 percent of the land, quickly displacing the production of food from the best land. Both sugar and tobacco were exported to the mainland. Puerto Rico was a raw-material-producing country with typical low wages and backward technology.

The *second* "development" took place throughout the 1950s, when the United States had a great abundance of capital and Puerto Rico became a "profit sanctuary," offering very attractive conditions for investors: tax exemption on property and income, low wages, low rents for industrial space, tax exemption on machinery and equipment imported from the U.S. and a strategic location near the United States. This was the time of Governor Luis Muñoz Marín and his "Operation Bootstrap." Puerto Rico became a center for clothing, textiles, leather and, to a lesser extent, electrical products, which were exported to the United States for "very minor final production activities," to be sold in the United States and European markets and sent back to Puerto Rico as "U.S. products" at very high prices compared with salaries. The Puerto Rican people were earning less than U.S. workers but paying more for the products, totally "imported" from the mainland. In the late 1950s United States supermarkets, drugstores, and department stores began an offensive to control retail sales in the island which accelerated the destruction of the remnants of agricultural production and the disappearance of small merchants, leading to increased prices.

The *third* stage in the "development" began in the 1960s, when products in Puerto Rico were no longer competitive with those from European markets. Light industries moved to new "profit sanctuaries" in the Dominican Republic and Taiwan, where there were lower wages than in Puerto Rico. Meanwhile, the island was being used as a midway center for refining petroleum and the production of petrochemical raw materials (61 percent of the gasoline and fuel oil re-exported to the U.S. and 95 percent of the petrochemical raw materials). Around $1.6 billion has been invested in the petrochemical and petroleum industry in 13 years, transforming Puerto Rico into the third largest petrochemical center in the world. In addition, $500 million has been invested in highly mechanized industries.

But these substantial investments have a seamy side to them. First, this new type of development has reduced the number of jobs absorbed by former industries and, on the other hand, has increased considerably the consumption of energy. The new industries are low-labor and energy-intensive. Puerto Rico is one of the areas of higher energy consumption in the world. "However," a Puerto Rican analyst has said:

> The new industries have not contributed to the island's economic growth as expected. Nor have they had significant impact in solving chronic local unemployment since these industries, while offering higher salaries, require fewer and more highly skilled workers per dollar goods produced on per dollar invested. At the present time, the local oil industry employs only 1 percent of the total labor force and generates only 5 percent of the island's income. On the other hand, it consumes 35 percent of the island's energy.[7]

On the other hand, the highly mechanized industries in Puerto Rico have affected fishing activities, agriculture and the health of the inhabitants. As Dr. Neftalí Garciá says, "During the last decade, capital investors have exported pollution from their countries to colonial and neo-colonial countries: we have called this *environmental colonialism.*" And the author is not mentioning another very touchy issue: the use of one of the islands as a target for the U.S. Marine's bombing range maneuvers.

So, through four-score years, Puerto Rico has been "developed" in such a way that it has been *producing what it does not consume, and consuming what it does not produce.* Profit is not precisely for the Puerto Rican people. Through "development of underdevelopment" Puerto Rico has become more and more dependent, exhausted and polluted.

Puerto Rican "dependence" on the U.S.A. is further illustrated by Father Alvaro de Boer, O.P., a Dutch Catholic missionary on the island:

At the present time, 80 percent of the Puerto Rican economy is controlled by the United States' multinational corporations. Twenty-four United States-owned chain stores are responsible for all sales. In addition, foreign capital, mostly from the United States, controls 81 percent of the manufacture; 100 percent air travel; over 50 percent of the insurance companies and over 60 percent of the financial operations. Ninety percent of the industrial products for exportations are generated by foreign industries, which means that the profits, for the most part, do not enter Puerto Rico's economy.

The amount and percentage of profits generated for the United States in Puerto Rico (from 13.8 to 46.6 percent in some industries) is almost unbelievable, according to the same source:

> In 1974 alone, the capital generated by investments in Puerto Rico and repatriated to the United States amounted to $1,345 million, almost 10 percent of all profits of the United States in the world(!) It means that Puerto Rico, with only 3.1 million inhabitants, is the fifth biggest market, customer, client, consumer or buyer of the United States products in the world: it spent $6.6 billion in purchases made in the United States in 1974 alone(!)[8]

Of course, all these profits go to big corporations based in the United States, but it is from the common taxpayer that resources are produced for welfare programs to compensate for the effects of unemployment, the high cost of living, and the low salaries of the island. While generating fortunes for the already rich, this "development" is expelling its own inhabitants out of the country through forced migration and contributing to generating the highest per capita crime rate in the world.

The "cry of my people" resounds with disenchantment from "the island of enchantment."

The Brazilian Miracle

One might think that a small island like Puerto Rico is more vulnerable to dependent development and less likely a prospect for a self-sustained development. According to World Bank President Robert McNamara, only "continent-countries" can be self-sufficient. If there is such a country in the world, it is Brazil, with its more than three million square miles, its huge seacoasts and strategic position, its enormous natural resources, its agriculture, mining, and industrial potential, and its dynamic 120 million people. And yet the "Brazilian miracle" of the last decade may be conclusive evidence of how elusive the goal of "development" is for Third World countries in the present global constellation. Or how high the social, human and national costs of such a goal may be.

What is the *Brazilian miracle?* It has been highly publicized as an outstanding success of development through foreign investments, a pure model of dependent capitalist development.

Nelson Rockefeller in his famous report of 1969 saw the solution of Latin American underdevelopment in two factors: 1) increase in foreign investments and private enterprise; 2) increase in military assistance for the Latin American armies and police forces. Both recommendations have been thoroughly and systematically applied in Brazil during the last fifteen years. So, if it has succeeded there, we have found the answer to Latin American underdevelopment.

In productivity or sheer economic growth, the figures are really impressive. Between 1968 and 1973 Brazil had a sustained GNP growth of 10 percent with a considerable increase in its industrial product, its export of manufactured products, and in international credit and financial reserves. Industry grew by an average of 11 percent a year. At the same time, inflation was kept at a stable level. Growth was particularly noticeable in high technology industries such as the automobile industry—up to one million cars a year—with its related industries and economic activities (parts, steel, glass, heavy petrochemistry, highways, construction, shopping centers) and of infrastructural services such as electric power, steel production, iron ore, cement, etc. This growth seemed to forecast the near-end of technological dependence. The economic boom was accompanied by a great flow of students into elementary and secondary schools and universities. New universities—mostly private—and massive graduate programs were created. Brazilian export growth was unprecedented: a six-fold increase in 11 years! Manufacturers' production doubled while coffee exports dropped, from 53 percent of the country's total exports to 23.8 percent.

Unpublicized Facts

There were, however, some unpublicized facts about the "miracle," such as the near zero growth of the clothing and shoe industries, the *decrease* in textile production during the same period, and the failure of social programs, such as housing and literacy plans. The increase of production and consumption was concentrated in a particular sector of society, the 20 percent minority at the top, while food and the basic commodities for the great majority of the population were inadequate. National income was massively concentrated in the top 5 percent income bracket who moved from a per capita income of $1,645 in 1960 to $2,940 in 1970, comparable to European levels. Fifteen percent also got an increase of $540 to $720 per capita income during the same time. The Catholic Bishops of the Northeast, however, denounced the *impoverishment* of the people in the midst of the "miracle" by quoting the following figures:

> Concentration of income has reached levels which reveal better than anything else the true meaning of the government's economic policy. Between 1960 and 1970, the 20 percent of the Brazilian population with the highest income raised its share in the national income from 54.4 percent to 64.1 percent, while the remaining 80 percent saw their share reduced from 45.5 percent to 36.8 percent. The imbalance is glaringly revealed in the fact that in 1970, the 1 percent group of the Brazilian population earned more than did half of the entire population.[9]

Even these figures do not show the real drama and the human cost of the so-called "miracle." It is not only a matter of approximate percentages of the total income but a matter of life and death for the lower 80 percent and the poorest among the poor in their midst. There is another cruel side to these figures, as the bishops said:

> What is very serious is that such an income concentration was made possible because the buying power of wages was brutally lowered. Between 1961 and 1970, the *decrease* of the real wage was about 38.3 percent. During the same period, the increase of average real productivity was 25.6 percent. For the realization of the so-called "Brazilian miracle," the government, through its regulation of minimum wages, has thus transferred part of the income of the working masses to the classes which are enjoying the fruits of economic growth.

Theotonio dos Santos, one of the leading Brazilian economists in exile whose information we have been using in this section, affirms that the official propaganda of the "miracle" has been trying to hide the "real misery" of the Brazilian people: "an increase in the rate of exploitation of Brazilian workers, increases in the duration of their working-days, decreases in their feeding and other essential consumption aspects, as well as increase in infant mortality rates."[10] One publication commented in 1977, "while the upper class lives in the First World, the masses are in the Third World."

So it becomes clear once again that economic growth does not necessarily mean human development. Not only that, but we can have an increase in the GNP while reducing the PCI of the vast majority of the people. And it becomes also crystal clear that the "trickle down" theory (let's improve the condition of those at the top and the benefits will trickle down to the majority at the bottom) is self-delusion or sheer hypocrisy.

The "cry of my people" wouldn't allow us to resort to either one with a clear conscience.

The Transnationals Enter the Picture

Some other aspects of the "Brazilian miracle" have not been publicized: the increase of imports in relation to the increase of exports, the role of the transnational corporations and the denationalization of Brazilian industry, the astronomical growth of the external debt and the social cost of the "miracle" in expanding poverty and inhuman repression.

The fabulous increase in imports was caused by the quadrupling of petroleum prices and related to the importation of technology at very high prices, the overbilling of transnational corporations in selling their products from abroad, and the underselling by the same corporations of their products to their parent or filial companies elsewhere. Last but not least is luxury imports for the high-income minorities with their new styles of consumption, made possible by increased income and stimulated by the transnational corporations through the overwhelming persuasive power of the media, which they also controlled. Celso Furtado has maintained, "The surplus of capital benefits only the proprietors of capital," and the affluent minority is the only one to have access to the new line of products available from internal or external markets. This is *modernization,* not development.[11]

Theotonio dos Santos concludes that "the Brazilian model is sunk in crisis": the annual growth rate of the GNP fell to 4 percent in 1975; and the external debt of the country is at bankruptcy while inflation continues to increase. "The 'miracle' is turned upside down: from economic wonder it has turned into economic disaster."

In conclusion, there has been development, but development for whom? In the final analysis, the major beneficiaries of the "miracle" are the transnational corporations, together with the top 5 percent income sector of the population. The transnational corporations dominate not only the export business but also the internal market. During this decade a denationalization of industrial, commercial, financial, and agricultural property has been under way. National industries have had to close shop or join—as subsidiaries or minor partners—to big foreign corporations. Besides, the transnational corporations control most of the assets in the following sectors:

1) Tobacco—93.7 percent of the assets of the 10 biggest enterprises in this sector;
2) Transportation materials—Eight TNCs control 89.7 percent of the assets;
3) Rubber products—Three TNCs control 81 percent of the assets;
4) Machinery—Seven TNCs control 72 percent of the assets;
5) Electric—equipment and communications—Six TNCs control 52.4 percent;
6) Textiles—Five TNCs control 55.4 percent of the assets;
7) Non-metallic minerals—Five TNCs control 52.4 percent of the assets.[12]

The following list will give an idea of the investments and returns of 10 of the transnational corporations working in Brazil in a 10-year period, 1965-1975 (in million dollars):

	Investment	Re-investment	Profit	Imported Technology Remittance	Total returns
Volkswagen	$119.5	$ 72.8	$ 70.6	$208.5	$279.1
Rhodia	14.3	108.7	39.9	20.7	60.6
Esso	1.8	67.7	44.5		44.5
Pirelli	28.7	37.8	45.1	19.8	64.9
Phillips	9.9	51.2	5.0	9.4	14.4
Firestone	4.1	44.5	48.1	2.1	50.2
General Electric	13.9	32.2	19.4	4.3	23.7
Souza Cruz	2.5	129.5	81.3	1.0	82.3
Johnson and Johnson	0.7	34.0	17.0	5.7	22.7
Anderson Clayton	1.4	28.2	16.8		16.8
Light (Canada)	102.0	85.4	114.7	0.6	115.3
TOTAL	298.8	692.0	502.4	272.1	774.5

(Source CPI, Multinationals)

To summarize the chart, in 10 years the corporations invested $298.8 million, with a *net profit* of $502.4 million; their *capital* was more than *tripled* by reinvestments of profits in the country, adding up to $692 million; with a return of $272.1 million through imported technology. The total return to the country of origin was $774.5 million.

Looking at this—which often is presented as "aid for development"—one has to ask, aid for whom? Development for whom? Michael Harrington, writing on "Why Poor Nations Stay Poor,"[13] affirms that, because of world economic structures after World War II, "poverty subsidizes affluence" through this dramatic phenomenon of "the flow of money from the poor to the rich." He quotes Chilean Chancellor Gabriel Valdés, who said at the White House in 1969:

> It is generally believed that our continent is receiving real aid in financial matters. The figures demonstrate the contrary. We can affirm that Latin America is contributing to financing the development of the United States and the other industrial nations(!)[14]

In Debt Without Buying

This incredible result of a decade of miraculous development is even more dramatic when the picture is completed with the increase of Brazil's external debt. At the peak of the "miracle" the external debt increased from $6.424 million in 1972 to a record of $45 billion in 1979, "a bankrupt situation," according to Brazilian economist Theotonio dos Santos. That astronomical figure represents more than four times the total value of Brazilian exports. To make things worse, in October 1978 financiers from Europe and the United States increased the interest rate from former loans from 7.5 percent to 12 percent, according to risks of the situation and the dollar devaluation. The weekly publication from São Paulo, *Movimento,* said with sour humor:

> ANOTHER HALF BILLION MORE:
> WHILE WE WORKED ON THE PRESENT EDITION
> WE BECAME MORE IN DEBT WITHOUT BUYING
> ANYTHING

Michael Harrington describes the situation as a vicious circle:

> A vicious circle is set in motion. Because of the losses suffered through the unfavorable terms of trade and the

outflow of profit and fees to the advanced economies, the Third World finds itself short of cash. Note that this is not because they have failed to produce substantial wealth. They have. Only, the structure of the world market has, by perfectly legal means, taken billions of that wealth away from them. So they have to borrow. In 1970, the underdeveloped countries had a net capital inflow of 2.6 billion dollars, but paid out 7.9 billion dollars on foreign investments. In short, they lost 5.3 billion.[15]

The "deterioration of the terms of trade" is another turn of the screw on Third World countries. Simply put, this means that while commodities from the Third World remain at a low price, fluctuating according to the convenience of the powers that control the world market, imported manufactures and technologies from the industrialized centers are continually on the rise. For instance, in 1970, Ecuador had to export *20* tons of bananas to buy a single tractor. In 1976, Ecuador had to export *60* tons of bananas to buy the same tractor. . . . So, when are we going to catch up with the game? Latin American countries lost $26.3 billion through this deterioration of the terms of trade between 1951 and 1966.

The Social Cost of Development

We have saved the reader from overwhelming references to human rights violations during the period of the "Brazilian miracle." It is enough to remember that the harshest repression began simultaneously with the economic boom in 1968. . . . Behind repression there is not only inhumanity and ideology but a specific model of development. As Christians we cannot stop with economic figures— no development whatsoever can be appraised without counting the human and social costs.

No wonder there is widespread pessimism, and even desperation, in Latin American countries about development after these three "decades of development."

A friend who read the first manuscript of this book after he had just spent four months in Brazil was surprised at the contrast of this gloomy picture and the impression he got from the people he met there. Yes, Brazil is a great country, full of contrasts, with a tremendous push for progress, with gigantic cities like São Paulo and futuristic metropolises like Brasilia. Yes, the Brazilian people are a great people, happy and proud. Just watch the multitudes in the crowded soccer stadiums cheering the three-time world champions, or the people dancing in the streets of Rio during carnival time. Stephan Zweig, the famous Austrian novelist, wrote a book after the Second World War with the prophetic title: *Brazil, the Country of the Future.* Brazilians have a reason to be proud: they have a huge country, with vast resources and a promising future. Many of them are enjoying life today.

But the Brazilian economists know this and much more, and they are concerned that the present trend cannot continue without mortgaging precisely that great future. The present Brazilian Government is also concerned and is trying seriously to correct the country's direction.*

The Catholic bishops and thousands of Christians who are in daily contact with the vast majority of the people, know what's below the surface. They know that the benefits of the "miracle" have reached only the tip of the iceberg, while the nine-tenths below the brilliant surface are still marginal, hungry, destitute, not receiving even the crumbs from the banquet. And, as we read in the document quoted in the preface, analyzing the situation in the Northeast, they have heard "the cry of my people."

We had better listen to that cry, not only to the self-congratulations of those who are in one way or another the beneficiaries of the present state of affairs.

What are we looking at? Mirage or reality?

To whom are we listening? The beneficiaries or the victims?

"The development of underdevelopment" has many mirages along the way.

---

*Brazilian President Figueiredo said recently: "Yes, the situation is very serious. We would lie if we said the contrary. A country that is going to spend 75 billion dollars buying oil and 8.5 billion paying its external debt (interests and payments) annually, and which wasn't able to export 14 billion, is not in an agreeable situation." (Quoted from "La revolución en jaque," Roberto Pombo, Inter-Press Service, *Presencia,* La Paz, September 10, 1979.)

4

HUMAN RIGHTS
A Decade of Captivity

We may not like what is going to be said in this chapter, but we dare not ignore it.

When President Carter in his inaugural message pledged, "Our commitment to human rights must have an absolute character," he touched a very sensitive chord in the Latin American situation. "The cry of my people" south of the Rio Grande—in countless jails, torture chambers, hideouts, or silenced forever in cemeteries, volcanoes, in the bottom of rivers or of the sea—was being heard from the mouth of the brand-new President of the United States. This time the dictators and repressive forces of many Latin American countries could not dismiss denunciation of human rights violations as "communist lies" or "terrorist tactics." They could not put those labels on the President of the United States.

According to Amnesty International—a nonpartisan agency promoting human rights, with headquarters in London and supporters and correspondents all over the world—during the last decade there have been hundreds of thousands of political prisoners, refugees, and exiles in Latin America; tens of thousands have been executed or tortured or assassinated; and 30,000 have "disappeared."

As after World War II the Nuremberg Trial uncovered the unbelievable crimes of Nazi Germany, one day we will be horrified to learn of the atrocities committed against tens of thousands of human beings and whole populations, right here, under our noses, inside our "inter-American system." And it will not be so easy to say that "we didn't know what was going on." Because we can know—if we want to.

59

The Hidden Will Be Uncovered

"There is nothing covered up which is not going to be exposed nor anything private which will not be made public," said Jesus (Matthew 10:26, Phillips). The process of uncovering has already begun in Latin America.

Orlando Letelier, ex-Chancellor of the Allende government and former Ambassador of Chile to the United States, was assassinated in Washington, D.C. A bomb put in his car killed him and a North American associate. It had been placed there by the long arm of the DINA (the secret police, the repressive apparatus of Pinochet's regime) and with the participation of anti-Castro Cuban exiles with CIA connections. The United States federal court uncovered the whole thing in a 21-day trial. The star witness was Michael Vernon Townley, an American resident in Chile, who confessed that he had put the bomb in Letelier's car on the instructions of DINA and with the cooperation of five Cuban exiles in the U.S.A. Three of them were convicted, and two others are fugitives. Townley got a lenient sentence for his cooperation with the prosecution in uncovering this international murder. According to Townley, General Manuel Contreras Sepúlveda, former chief of DINA, had ordered this assassination because Letelier, a socialist, was considered a dangerous opponent of General Augusto Pinochet's military regime. Townley himself had no regrets: "He was a soldier, I was a soldier."

The other defendants, whose extradition has been requested by the U.S. Justice Department and denied by Chilean authorities, were released in October 1979. But, thanks to international pressure, this secret plot was partially uncovered.[1]

Another sensational discovery in Chile was the macabre finding on December 7, 1978, of 27 corpses inside an abandoned limekiln in Talagante, 25 miles from Santiago. The information came out through private confession and was passed to Bishop Monsignor Enrique Alvear, with proper authorization from the anonymous confessor. The Catholic hierarchy, in turn, denounced it to the Supreme Court. Bishop Alvear himself was present with the authorities during the dreadful exhumation of the bodies from the 11-yard-long furnace. The bodies were found stashed below stones, lime and cement. The bodies showed signs of torture and bullet holes in the skulls. Fifteen were identified. The task of identification was not an easy one because the repressive tactics used on the people included the changing of identities, burning all identity documents and cutting off the fingers from the hands. But finally truth prevailed, and a military jury charged eight military police agents with "unnecessary violence," provoking the deaths of 15 peasant union members in 1973.

From September 11, 1973, the date of the military coup in Chile, up to 1977, at least 100,000 people had been subjected to arrest and detention, more than 5,000 had been executed, 2,500 had "disappeared," and tens of thousands had fled from Chile for political reasons.

But there are many other Pinochetist cemeteries to be uncovered. A few weeks after the coup of September 11, 1973, which overthrew the legal government of President Salvador Allende, the military junta prohibited fishing in the southern zone lakes. Reasons were not given, but fishermen knew why: they themselves had found human corpses in their nets. Two years later, while doing training exercises in the northern zone, the Chilean skindiving champion Raúl Choque discovered a huge underwater cemetery at the bottom of the sea. He was so impressed with what he saw that he committed the "imprudence" of talking about it. A few days later he was found dead in his home, and the authorities prevented an autopsy.[2]

Chile: Not Becoming Accustomed to Repression

The relatives of the "disappeared" started a hunger strike, supported by solidarity strikes in 19 other countries around the world, demanding information. An international delegation was organized to go to Chile in an attempt to assist the strikers in eliciting a response from the Chilean military government. One of the members of that delegation was Dorothee Sölle, a distinguished and world-renowned German theologian. Her report gives us some hints as to the tragedy of the "disappeared" and the spirit of resistance among the Chilean people.[3]

One of the political prisoners gave Dr. Sölle a silver coin as a gift. Written on it was a line from a poem by Pablo Neruda, "as if it were possible to imprison the air." "For me," says the German theologian, "this line offered a minimum categorical imperative for solidarity: not under any circumstances, especially any corruption, can we allow ourselves to get used to what has happened and what continues to happen." The Chilean people have not become accustomed to repression—and they have not forgotten their disappeared loved ones.

One morning while Dorothee Sölle was at one of the churches, where the strikers were lying down next to one another in two long rows on the floor, a delegation of medical students arrived to deliver a declaration of solidarity with more than 1,000 signatures. All of those

"This bitterness, is it hate?" by Solón.

who signed knew they were risking expulsion from the university, but they came singing to the church.

There was not only tragic loyalty, but also a good fighting mood and even humor among the strikers. In the Church of Jesús Obrero, the birthday of a hunger striker was celebrated by shaping a large cake from toilet paper and putting candles on it. More than 100 letters and telegrams in support of the strike were being received each day from people around the world.

> This strike is necessary in order for the country to grow, to move out of this phase of militarism that we are in. Half the population is caught up in guilt for having kept silent, for having tried to forget, or for being frightened. Now we are experiencing an awakening—it is in the midst of this people's movement that we can begin to do theology. This hunger strike is the *"locus theologicus"* (the place where theology is done).[4]

Dorothee Sölle reflects finally that "the Chileans are not as the majority of Germans under nazism"—they are still not accustomed to hearing about disappearances, to discovering mutilated corpses in their rivers, to accepting the harshness of the militarism which controls their lives. They continue resisting, struggling, searching.

This is "the cry of my people": the silent cry of the dead and "disappeared," the long-suffering cry of their loved ones.

In the Beginning Was Brazil

The infamous story of repression began in Brazil in 1964 with the military coup that overthrew the legal government of Joao Goulart. The military regime, in the biggest country in Latin America, has been in control for 15 years, reaching its peak of violence and terror in 1968. Gary McEoin, a keen observer of the Latin American scene from the United States who has made extended visits to the South, wrote in the early '70s that he believed Brazil was probably the best country to study as an illustration of current developments and that it represented the direction in which the continent was moving. The last tragic decade has proved that he was right.

McEoin himself summarized the situation in 1964 this way:

> Alarmed by the growing gap between the impoverished rural Northeast and the industrialized South, former presidents, Quadros and Goulart, favored projects to correct that

situation. They proposed to modernize agriculture by means of farm cooperatives and large state farms. Many of the new industrialists became frightened; alarmed at the growing role of the state, the increased taxes and the inflation, they moved closer to the landowners in opposition. This in turn drove the government further toward revolutionary change, seeking the support of the popular forces aroused by the prospect of active participation in public affairs. It proclaimed goals of land and income redistribution, economic nationalism, nationalization of large sectors of production, political mobilization of the urban and rural masses, and international neutralism and nonalignment. This, in turn, frightened the policy-makers of the United States and, with official encouragement, a coalition of politicians, businessmen, and the military, overthrew President Goulart in 1964.[5]

At the beginning the military regime was relatively restrained, and many citizens who had been pressed by galloping inflation under Goulart, including the vast majority of churchmen, supported the coup. But,

On one issue, the new regime was adamant from the outset. The whole process of stirring up the people had to stop. Francisco Juliao and his peasant leagues were wiped out. The parallel Christian trade unions were emasculated. Celso Furtado (economist) and Paulo Freire (pedagogue) were stripped of their rights as citizens and exiled, soon to be joined by . . . most of the country's intellectual leaders. The Basic Education Movement was seriously hit. Many schools were closed immediately and leaders arrested. . . . All student movements were banned. . . .[6]

The military government had promised a quick return to constitutional government, but it had to undo the policies and programs of the ousted government. So,

Laws providing for the distribution of certain non-cultivated lands to peasants were annulled. In return for the United States' support and its promises of major loans, the regulations limiting the export of business profits were withdrawn, and nationalization of oil refineries was restricted. Control of wages reduced the inflation rate without a serious reduction in business profits.[7]

A New Order: Consensus by Repression

Then the establishment of a new order began through "institutional acts," decrees which were above the Constitution and the law of the country. Act No. 1 suspended constitutional guarantees and increased the power of the executive. Mass arrests followed. The three previous presidents and many political leaders were stripped of their political rights for 10 years. Close to 5,000 people were punished by "revolutionary" decrees and forced to disband. Congress was purged of 112 members, and several state governors were deposed. Two thousand military men were retired. Thousands of military commissions of inquiry were created with judicially uncontrolled powers. Institutional Act No. 2 dissolved all political parties and created two new ones—the government party and a "loyal opposition party"—under rigid government control and according to its rules of the game. The purged Congress had to "elect" the President of the Republic and state governors. In 1967, a new Constitution was promulgated, incorporating the "institutional Acts" and authorizing the President to promulgate new laws without consulting Congress. A press censorship law and a national security law followed, whereby all opposition was treated as treason in military courts.

Any movement—political parties, student or workers' organizations—had to operate underground. Extreme right-wing organizations responded with assassination and torture. The military regime was caught on a treadmill, trying to reconcile its policies of economic modernization with the preservation of political and social immobility. It decided for an increase in repression. This was the beginning of a spiral of terror and violence.

Issued in December 1968, Institutional Act No. 5, a sort of "coup within the coup," gave the President unlimited dictatorial power, allowing him to recess the National Congress and all legislatures, to oust and appoint governors and city mayors, to suspend the rights of any citizens for 10 years, to prohibit trade union or political activity, to subject citizens to police surveillance and confinement, to dismiss any public employee, and to suspend habeas corpus. In 1969 the President was elected by the 239 senior officers of the armed forces, Congress having been recessed by the former President. His election was later confirmed by the several-times-purged Congress, called back into session.

Between 1964 and 1969, no fewer than 30,000 persons had been arrested on charges of subversion, and 12,000 of them were jailed but never tried (their average age, including that of women and young

"Death in the valley" by Solōn.

girls, was 22 years). Repression was becoming commonplace and systematic. During this period the government mounted strong campaigns against the church and its more outspoken representatives.[8]

Torture

By 1970, the issue of torture was becoming critical in Brazil. Unknown to the vast majority of the population, silenced by the censored press, and denied by the authorities and great sectors of the church at the time, it began to be known outside Brazil. Massive dossiers, clandestinely compiled and smuggled out of the country by outlawed citizens and priests and nuns, were reaching the Vatican, the World Council of Churches and the Congress of the United States. They revealed not merely incidental excesses of functionaries but a definite pattern of incredible dehumanizing repression.

A committee of scholars, writers, religious leaders and spokespersons for civil liberties in the United States issued a report in April 1970, concluding that the use of torture in Brazil "now appears to surpass all other techniques of police investigation and inquiry. Torture has become so commonplace that the three armed services have organized courses." The report refers to a class in torture conducted in October 1969 at the headquarters of the state police of Minas Gerais, in Belho Horizonte, where twelve male political prisoners were used as guinea pigs. Here is the description made in a collective document of the victims:

> On October 8, a class in interrogation was held . . . for a group of about a hundred military men, the majority of them sergeants from the three branches of the armed forces. Just before the class, Mauricio (de Paiva) was given electric shocks "to see if the equipment was in good working order," in the words of a private named Mendoca. At about 4 p.m., just before the class was to begin, the (following ten) prisoners were led up to the classroom where the session was already in progress: Mauricio de Paiva, Angelo Pezzutti, Murilo Pinto, Pedro Paulo Bretas, Alfonso Celso Lara, Nilo Sergio, Julio A. Antonio, Irany Campos, and a former MP from Guanabara and another prisoner known as Zezinho. Immediately after, they were ordered to enter the room and strip. While Lieutenant Haylton was showing slides and explaining each type of torture, its characteristics and effects, Sergeant Andrade, Oliveira, Rossoni, and Rangel, together with Corporals Mendoca and (illegible name) and the soldier

Marcelino were torturing the prisoners in the presence of the hundred military men in a "live" demonstration of the various torture methods in use. Mauricio suffered electric shocks, Bretas had a finger put in irons, Murilo suffered to stand on top of cutting edges of tin cans, Zezinho was hung from the "pau de arara" and the ex-MP was clubbed, while Nilo Sergio had to hold his balance on one foot while heavy weights hung from his outstretched arms.[9]

The previously quoted report from a committee in the U.S. says that since September 1969, "United States security agents flood Brazil." In August 1970, an Italian Catholic magazine, *Il Regno* of Bologna, published a report from a correspondent who testified that he was one of a group of political prisoners who had been tortured "by Brazilian police and an unknown group of people who spoke only English." McEoin adds the comments that two of the instructors in torture had non-Brazilian names: Lieutenant Haylton and Sergeant Rangel. Dan Mitrione, the instructor of Uruguayan torturers executed by the "Tupamaros," had worked before as an internal security expert in Belho Horizonte and Rio de Janeiro. The United States military mission to Brazil, the biggest in Latin America, was training 2,255 Brazilians in interrogation of prisoners and other techniques of guerrilla warfare between 1964 and 1968.

The uncovering process in Brazil has already begun. After 15 years of strict censorship of the press, there is a growing freedom, and stories from the dark days of repression are beginning to appear in the leading Brazilian newspapers. Some outstanding national figures have seen their political rights restored and many who were exiled for years have been allowed to return. In spite of a very special electoral law, the opposition almost won the majority in Congress. The present President, Joao Baptista Figueiredo, has promised that "democratization" will take place during his term, and a few months after his inauguration a limited amnesty for political prisoners was approved (excluding those charged of terrorism or bloody political actions). Still it is purposely a "restricted democracy," depending on "good behavior," according to President Figueiredo, but the process is opening up.

If Brazil represents the direction in which the continent is moving, there is hope that "the cry of my people" will finally be heard.

The Pattern Extends to the Andes

In August 1971 it was the turn of Bolivia, Brazil's southwestern neighbor in the high Andes mountains. Bolivia in 1952 had the second greatest revolution in Latin America of this century (the first one was in Mexico in 1910 and the third one in Cuba in 1959). It was a great step forward, taking the country out of feudalism through the nationalization of the big mines, an agrarian reform and universal suffrage. The army was dissolved in 1952 but, reconstituted with the help of the U.S.A., it again took the reins in 1964.

In 1970-71, in the midst of serious economic troubles, a nationalist progressive sector of the army tried to give a new economic turn to the nation by nationalizing the Gulf Oil Company installations and the big zinc mine Matilde, under concession to the Phillips Corporation. A popular movement, including miners, urban workers, students, and some Christian groups, began to take shape and to participate in General J. J. Torres' regime, pressing him for more radical measures. Another military movement, lead by General Hugo Banzer, with open support from private businesses and the incidental participation of sectors of two traditional parties, ousted Torres and initiated a new regime. The United States backed the new coup, though material and financial support was channelled through Brazil, which provided armaments for the adventure. International loans which had been held for months under Torres' government flooded into Bolivia immediately after the coup.

Repression of workers, students and peasants was quick and drastic, particularly in the economically booming area of Santa Cruz. Torture, prison and political exile were not new in Bolivian political history, but this time they were openly employed. Compared with the Brazilian and Chilean records, Bolivian repression looks mild. Any opposition, however, was repressed; no dissent was allowed. Over 20,000 Bolivians had to flee to other countries.

The Ministry of Interior's political control was thoroughly efficient. Politicians, labor leaders, student leaders, priests and nuns who had been engaged in social programs were expelled from the country. Even the ex-Minister of the Interior, Andrés Selich, one of the architects of the 1971 coup, was stabbed to death by government thugs. A few months later, several hundred unarmed peasants in the Valley of Cochabamba protested the increased cost of living. A hundred of them were killed by the army, who the peasants thought were coming only to dialogue on behalf of the government. This is known as "The Massacre of the Valley" or "the Tolata massacre."[10]

Today Bolivia is one of the first nations in Latin America initiating a process of "democratization" and transition to civil order. The uncovering has just begun, and the new Congress is calling former President Hugo Banzer to account for his regime.

The Pattern Moves South

Uruguay has been known as the "Switzerland of America" because of its democratic spirit, its freedoms, its social legislation and its high level of education. Today it might be called "the jail of America." What has happened?

During the last decade Uruguay has been passing through serious economic troubles. Exports—traditionally based on meat and wool—could no longer permit the welfare state to play the role of Providence in a country where most of the population were public servants or social security beneficiaries from the state. There was no economic alternative offered. The oligarchies seized power again, and Uruguay survives through repression.

According to Joseph Comblin, the downfall of the economic system brought forth the downfall of democracy. And what precipitated the downfall of democracy was the way in which the unrest of the opposition was provoked by the urban guerrillas or "Tupamaros." They began, Robin Hood-style, to help the poor, unmasking the operations of some of the national corporations. They performed spectacular actions and seemed unconquerable. One of those spectacular actions was the kidnapping of the American CIA agent and secret police advisor Dan Mitrione. He was accused of teaching all the methods perfected by the CIA in Vietnam and of having participated personally in "interrogations" of political prisoners who had been tortured. He was "judged" by the movement and finally executed.[11]

The state's repressive action began with President Jorge Pacheco Areco from 1968 to 1972. Pacheco organized the army, geared to anti-revolutionary action with the help of American and Brazilian instructors. Under the next President, José María Bordaberry, the army succeeded in destroying the "Tupamaro" movement. By then the army was the decisive power and the President a figurehead. In 1973, Congress was closed and the Constitution annulled. Uruguay became a "national security" state.

Uruguay has the dubious record of being the most repressive country in the world, "giving it the distinction of having the highest concentration per capita of political prisoners." According to Amnesty International's estimates, one of every 450 people in Uruguay is a Prisoner of Conscience; approximately one out of every 50 citizens has suffered interrogation, temporary arrest, or imprisonment. Another revealing statistic is that from 1973-1978, about 700,000 Uruguayans left the country (25 percent of a total population of 2,800,000), mostly young people, workers, technicians and professionals; "the living forces of Uruguay." In that same period, 50,000 Uruguayans were imprisoned and half of them savagely tortured. By the beginning of 1979, there were 6,000 political prisoners in Uruguay. The political rights of more than 39,000 citizens have been legally denied. Entire libraries have been burned.

The "new order" has closely copied the Brazilian model: military control, Congressional recess, prohibition of political parties, abolition of labor unions, press censorship, executive decrees over and above the constitution, military control of the universities, consensus by repression, militarized justice, torture. The same anti-communist creed, the same "national security" ideology, the same psychosis of "total war" against the "subversives," the same careful and systematic destruction of all democratic structures and of all human rights of dissidents.

A Christian Officer and Torture

The following letter is a response to letters Amnesty International has sent to numerous middle-level Uruguayan officials, and it is addressed to the Pope:

> I know that I am taking a great risk, and that for some of my fellow officers this will be treason, but nobody can ask me to forget my Christian faith, my respect for the human being.

> To this letter I attach two photographic proofs of what I say: both were taken in one of the many private houses that are being used for torture, one called the "banner" *(la bandera),* the other called the "sawhorse" *(el caballete).**

> The Uruguayan armed forces systematically torture and maltreat political or trade union detainees. I have hundreds of proofs, from my own painful personal experience.

> The photograph of the "banner" was taken after the prisoner had been hanging for three hours, under a sun over 90°F. (28° C.) and he was undoubtedly left there for many more long hours.

> There are many variants of torture and of disgusting names: the "submarine" *(el submarino),* near suffocation by immersion in basins of water, or with nylon bags, or a

---

*These pictures have been exhibited during hearings in the U.S. Congress, House Sub-Committee on International Organizations, June 17, July 27-28, Aug. 4, 1976.

combination of both forms. I know several cases of death, including young people. The hooding of all prisoners for an indefinite period; the interminable periods that detainees, male and female, have to spend standing, naked, suffering severe beatings, and forced to carry out their physiological needs still standing.

The "sawhorse" consists of a sharp metal bar, with an edge on which prisoners are seated handcuffed and naked for hours, with their feet hanging in the air.

There are many variants of the use of electricity. The electric prod *(la picana)*, applied to the limits of resistance (I have seen prisoners with serious inflammation and infection of the prostate and testicles).

The "telephone" *(el teléfono)* is the application of a cable to each earlobe. I have seen the strongest officers and non-commissioned officers selected to punish prisoners, with clubs, pipes, karate blows. And I can state that no one is safe from this treatment; some cases are more brutal than others, but practically all prisoners, irrespective of age or sex, are beaten and tortured. Dozens of prisoners have been taken to the Military Hospital with fractures and lesions. Such a level of sadism has been reached that military doctors supervise the torture.

The *women* are a separate category. The officers, non-commissioned officers and the troops greet the arrival of young women detainees with delight. Some even come in to take part in interrogations on their days off. I have personally witnessed the worst aberrations committed with women, in front of other prisoners, by many interrogators. Many of the women prisoners are only held for the purpose of discovering the whereabouts of their husband, father or son, that is, they themselves have been accused of nothing.

I could continue, but I suppose that to provoke the same disgust that I feel, this is sufficient. . . .

I am sending this letter to everybody who can do anything to free us from this nightmare, in which we are all prisoners. I am addressing this letter in particular to the Holy See, since the only thing which has carried me through the nightmare is my profound faith that sooner or later the justice of God will come to my country.[12]

"The cry of my people" is sounding this time through the sensitive conscience of one of the servants in the court of Pharaoh, in a tiny country that had—and deserves—a better destiny in the family of American nations.

The situation in Uruguay became so outrageous that the Carter Administration picked Uruguay, together with Ethiopia and Argentina, as its first symbolic action in favor of human rights, reducing the military assistance to these countries. Ironically, however, the Uruguayan police have been subsidized and trained by the United States Government, with an additional loan for $30 million.[13]

In hearing the outcry of the tortured, we should remember what Jeri Laber said in the September 25, 1976, *Washington Post:* "To know that torture exists anywhere in the world and not to act is also dehumanizing."

Terror Reaches Argentina

Terror has reached Argentina, one of the most civilized, well-educated and politically sophisticated countries in our hemisphere. As in other countries, trouble started at the economic roots, spread through the political spectrum, exploded in the social unrest of the masses, and reached its critical point in guerrilla warfare, terrorism and repression. The military junta that came to power in 1976, formed by three chiefs of the armed forces and presided over by General Jorge Videla, succeeded in repressing the guerrillas in the north of the country and subversive actions in the cities. But the price was too high. It was combating terror with terror. The para-military and para-police apparatus continued under the new regime. As in Brazil, the terrorist counter-guerrilla or counter-subversion groups were not easy to disband. Violence bred violence, and terror bred terror.

The Argentine record on human rights violations during the government of the present military junta is shattering: 15,000 disappeared; 10,000 political prisoners; tens of thousands expatriated; 4,000 killed. In just one year, 7,000 habeas corpus petitions were denied. The few lawyers who dared to present cases of the victims of repression were kidnapped and "disappeared." Ten priests were murdered and more than 30 journalists were kidnapped or killed.

Again, the Carter Administration, with the support of Congress, chose to reduce military assistance to Argentina on the grounds of gross violation of human rights. President Carter has sent his own representative on human rights; and Amnesty International has done the same. Later on the Organization of American States sent a commission, and thousands of relatives of prisoners and disappeared ones *queued* to complain and make inquiries about their dear ones.

The report of the commission has been withheld so far. But President Videla keeps saying that there are no political prisoners in Argentina and that those who have died or disappeared were members of the guerrilla and subversive groups who died in confrontations with the forces of order. Among the 14 different police and military security forces there are no official records of detainees. Many times the police simply applied *la ley de fuga* (the law of escape), killing people from behind as if they were escaping. Or, after torturing to death or executing prisoners, they publish in the press that there was an encounter between the police or the army with a guerrilla group, and that so and so among the subversives died in the encounter. Such was the case of Elizabeth Käsemann, the daughter of the famous German New Testament scholar, Ernst Käsemann.

Murder in Argentina

The story of Elizabeth Käsemann has been carefully told by Elaine Magalis in *The Christian Century*.[14] "Elizabeth was an attractive, bright, sensitive and adventurous young woman, and Argentina was a stopping-off place on a youthful pilgrimage," says Magalis. Elizabeth, like many other European students, was very much interested in Latin America and was officially registered as a student in economics at the Buenos Aires University. Diana Houstoun, her Argentine friend of British ancestry, was studying theology at Union Theological Seminary. According to Diana's witness, both of them were in contact with other students and, like students all over the world, they participated in demonstrations. They read and talked about politics and the theology of liberation. But, as Argentine political regimes became more repressive, the political interest of the two friends began to wane. "We still had certain relationships with people," says Diana Houstoun, "and I think some kind of ideological inclination, but we weren't active participants in any political movements at that time."

On June 1, 1976, the usual armed forces communique announced: "Sixteen left-wing guerrillas . . . killed during an army raid in Monte Grande." It named only one of the dead: Elizabeth Käsemann, a foreign national." The Argentine government claimed that Elizabeth's death took place on May 24 in a gun battle with Montoneros—urban guerrillas—in the provincial town of Monte Grande. Dr. Käsemann, her father in Germany, was not officially notified until June 6 and, curiously, the death certificate was not filled out until June 8. The autopsy performed on her exhumed body in Tübingen three weeks after her death found that she had been machine-gunned in the back. One bullet hole was found in the back of the neck and another in the heart. "This is the way executions are done," says Dr. Käsemann. An article in *Evangelische Kommentar* states that according to "reliable sources . . . she was caught in a trap, after which she was tortured for several days, and with the highest probability held as a political prisoner for 11 weeks in the First Army Command in the barracks of Palermo."

Why was Elizabeth killed? We may never know. The Argentine Government, finally responding to Dr. Käsemann, added to its version of the killing a recital of Elizabeth's alleged activities in underground organizations, including the Trotskyite Fourth International. The military claimed that she had been the leader of one such organization and had been involved in assassinations during guerrilla raids. William Wipfler of the National Council of Churches office on human rights muses that "at some point repressive governments like Argentina's probably believe their own stories. . . . They create their own paranoia." But it will be difficult for the rest of the world to believe this story. Maybe one day the secret will be uncovered. The article quoted suggests two other possible reasons for Elizabeth's murder: Her captors were more afraid of the furor that might be created by what she would say on her release than they were of any publicity attendant to her death. Or, possibly, there was an effort to hide irremediable damage—physical or mental—done to her.

These uncertainties are part of the horror of inhuman repression and part of "the cry of my people."

Dr. Ernst Käsemann in an essay concludes:

> My point is not to seek revenge for my daughter. I do not want to envision and defend her as a martyr. However, I should like her best to open people's eyes so that the reality of Argentina, so beautiful and yet harboring an inferno, can be seen. I should not like to leave the last word to the executioners and the military.[15]

From Land of Refuge to Hunting Ground

A sacred and most respected right in Latin American tradition has been *el derecho de asilo* (the right of asylum), by which any Latin American country had to give refuge and to protect the life of a political refugee from any other Latin American country. This right was respected throughout our history, by any regime even in the most difficult times. What has happened in this decade of captivity in Latin

America, however, is that refugees do not find the protection from persecuting authorities they seek in other countries. Instead they find the coordination of intelligence services, a cooperation between repressive agencies of different countries, an international exchange of prisoners, arrest by proxy and killing by request. From a land of refuge, Latin America has become a hunting ground where exiles, political refugees and prisoners are political targets anywhere, hunted like rabbits by secret police.

The situation in Argentina after the death of President Perón was particularly dramatic because the 15,000 refugees from neighboring countries were suddenly caught in the trap of right-wing terrorism under Isabel Perón and later on under the military junta. General Carlos Prats, former Minister of Defense of the Allende Government in Chile, was assassinated in the streets of Buenos Aires. Juan José Torres, ex-President of Bolivia, a progressive nationalist and a very tolerant ruler himself, was murdered and thrown out on the streets of Buenos Aires. Zelmar Michelini and Héctor Gutiérrez Ruiz, moderate democratic members of the Uruguayan Senate, were also kidnapped and killed with total impunity, and with the open complicity of the Argentine police.[16] The journalist and writer Rodolfo Walsh, now "disappeared," said that the federal police had been conducted by officers who had received scholarships and training by the CIA through the Agency for International Development and who act under the authority of the CIA station chief in Argentina.

Disappeared Children—in the International Year of the Child. . . .

Even children are not respected in this international traffic of prisoners. They are used to pressure their parents, who are imprisoned and tortured. And when parents are killed, children disappear. . . . The kidnapping of Uruguayan children (there are full lists of names, giving particular circumstances) is something that should stir the conscience of the world.

Ironically, in the International Year of the Child (1979), Cardinal Archbishop of Brazil, Dom Paulo Evaristo Arns, and Rev. James Wright of the Presbyterian Church in Brazil have denounced to the international press agencies and through them to the rest of the world the existence of 99 children who have "disappeared" from three neighboring countries: Argentina, Uruguay and Brazil. They include 21 babies and 24 adolescents who were with their parents at the moment of kidnapping and 54 babies born in confinement to women who were pregnant when kidnapped. So far no word has been received about their whereabouts.

"The cry of my people" is also the cry of these innocent and defenseless children which becomes the angry cry of our Lord, saying:

> If anyone leads astray one of these little children who believe in me, he would better be thrown into the depths of the sea with a millstone hung around his neck! Alas for the world with its pitfalls. . . . (Matthew 18:6-7)

The Pattern Moves North

On human rights the record of other Latin American countries is not very clean either. *Paraguay* has been under a legal dictatorship for more than a quarter of a century. General Alfredo Stroessner uses well-known tactics of repression, even against the church. *Peru,* in the last years of its nationalistic military revolution, has been hard on labor unions, students and peasant organizations. *Colombia,* under civilian governments, has a record of 500 peasants assassinated in three years (1975-1977) and 243 people kidnapped by clandestine, unconstitutional police bodies and held in jails and military camps.[18] Amnesty International has reported 20,000 assassinated (mostly peasants) by para-military groups since 1966. Even Mexico, the most stable country in the southern hemisphere, has not been free from the repression of workers' movements. In 1968 an awful mass killing of university students took place in Tatlelolco, a kind of Kent State episode multiplied a hundred times. In *El Salvador,* peasants and priests have been murdered by para-police organizations, following step by step the pattern of the "southern cone" model.

The classic example of hideous dictatorship in Central America has been the Somoza regime in Nicaragua, supported by military assistance from the United States Government and holding power through the savage repression of the National Guard, which ended with the triumphant revolution of 1979. But it left behind 30,000 dead, 40,000 orphans, 600,000 destroyed homes, and a whole country in shambles.

Uncovering is also happening in *Central America.* Events are not public, are not remembered, but there are some who know and will remember, for instance, what happened in *Guatemala.* Somebody rented a house and wanted to plant roses in the garden. But when digging he found not shells or diamonds but human bones; rings belonging to the dead, married couples; shoes of people buried alive.

That orchard had been the private cemetery of the former tenant, a "five-star official killer." It is also known that a whole group of top leaders of a political party in Guatemala were kidnapped while they were in session, including the women who were making coffee in the kitchen and children sitting in their laps. Nothing has been heard of them since. According to Amnesty International, 20,000 have been killed in Guatemala since 1966, the last 2,000 between 1978 and 1979.

The great Colombian writer, Gabriel Garciá Marquez, referring to the above nightmare of horrors, warns us, "Let's keep the watch against forgetfulness."[19]

National Security Ideology

In all these cases there is a common pattern, a common network of repression, a common strategy and, behind it all, a common ideology—the ideology of "national security."

The national security ideology is not a matter of simple brutality and pathological behavior. It is a matter of war. Lt. Col. Hugo Hildebrando Pascarelli of Argentina expressed it, "The struggle we are in doesn't know moral or natural limits, it is beyond good and evil."[20]

The essential concepts of the national security ideology are: the individual person does not exist, people are myths. What really exist are nations. But the nation is interchangeable with the state. Without the state, the nation is nothing. And the state is embodied in the government.

The state is an organ which has to defend itself, to strengthen itself and to be combative. Expanding nations, looking for vital space, have to be in a state of *permanent war:* war against the individual adversary, war against outside powers or ideologies, war against communism. The war is *total:* it mobilizes all citizens, civil and military; all peoples and countries are involved. All human activities are acts of war. The enemy has infiltrated everywhere.

General Videla, President of Argentina, said, "If obliged to, in Argentina, all the necessary persons will die in order to achieve the security of the nation."[21]

National Security doesn't ask about means, violent or nonviolent. National security is *absolute.*

National security makes no distinction between internal or external policy: the enemy is inside or outside the country. There is no difference between the army or the police, for they face the same problem, they fight the same enemy. The police exist not to protect citizens but to protect "the system."[22]

Where did we get this doctrine? It is not so new. It was the Nazi ideology of the state, and it was in Germany that the science of "geo-politics" was born. Later the French followed the doctrine in their colonial war against Algeria. And it is the doctrine adopted by the United States after the Second World War to justify participation in wars outside the United States, as a means of protecting "national security" at large. It was the rationale for the Vietnam adventure. It was the "ultima ratio" for Watergate, the ideology justifying the "Imperial Presidency" with its eavesdropping, wiretapping and stonewalling. It is the ideology behind CIA activities at home and abroad.[23]

This doctrine, of course, is taught in military training institutions, including the National War College, the Industrial College of the Armed Forces, and the Interamerican Defense College, all three located in Washington, D.C. It is taught in the strategic U.S. Army School of the Americas and other military schools located in the Panama Canal Zone. It is taught in the Superior School of War of Brazil, the National School of War of Argentina, the Superior Academy of National Security in Chile, and the Schools of High Military Studies in Ecuador, Peru and Bolivia.[24]

The Latin American military have proved to be advanced students, carrying the ideology to its ultimate consequences. While in the United States the National Security Council is in civilian hands, in Latin America it is totally in military hands. While in the United States national security is incarnated in the industrial-military complex and applied through foreign policy around the world, in Latin America it has been incarnated in the most inhuman repressive apparatus and applied against individual dissidents and social movements.

Still, it is the same ideology, and it may be good for our American friends to see its final effects in our dreadful experience south of the Rio Grande.

As Christians we cannot be indifferent to the existence of such a powerful instrument that puts human beings at the service of war machines and makes them mere objects of totalitarian ideologies of world leadership, world domination or so-called national security. In our Christian perspective, as in the best ideals of the American Dream, man comes first and foremost. Human rights are at stake around the whole world and in our three Americas.

Trilateralism: The New Ideology

There are indications, however, that this doctrine is being adjusted. The Trilateral Commission, made up of top businessmen, technologists, scholars and government representatives from Western Europe, Japan and the United States, are more concerned with what they call "a new international order," assuring raw materials for the industrialized world and their own leading roles in the world economy. David Rockefeller was one of its founders, Zbigniew Brzezinski one of its top brains, and Jimmy Carter a member before he became a candidate for the presidency of the United States. His "think tank" is made up mostly of members from the Trilateral Commission. For the latter the military model is becoming inadequate for the expanding world market and even a hindrance in facing the crisis of recession and inflation in the capitalistic world. Brzezinski's model of "restrained democracy" is now the trial balloon. We in Latin America are beginning to pass through a process of "democratization," as can be seen by the transition from military to civil governments in Ecuador and Bolivia, and the melting of the ice in Brazil. Even Chile, Argentina and Uruguay are trying to obtain good behavior certificates on human rights and are preparing for a transition from military to civil rule in a couple of years—with assurances that changes will not be too radical. The human rights campaign can be seen in the context of the new Trilateral strategy.*

---

*For those interested in knowing more about the Trilateral Commission, we suggest the following introductory readings:

A. Publications by the Trilateral Commission
   —*Task Force Reports:* 1-19, New York University Press, 1977.
   —*Trialogue* (Can be requested from: The Trilateral Commission, 345 East 46th St., New York, N.Y. 10017.
B. Books
   Brzezinski, Zbigniew: *Between Two Ages,* Penguin Books, 1970.
   Samuel P. Huntingdon, *The Crisis of Democracy*
C. Articles
   —Bird, Kai; "Trilateralism Goes to Work," *The Nation,* April 9, 1977.
   —Bliss, Shepherd; "Jimmy Carter: Trilateralism in Action," *The Guardian,* February 16, 1977.
   —Gelb, Leslie H.; "Brzezinski Viewed as Key Advisor to Carter," *The New York Times,* October 6, 1976.
   —Graider, William; "Trilateralists to Abound in Carter's White House," *Washington Post,* January 16, 1977.
   —Lewis, Paul; "A White House Supply Depot: The Trilateral Commission," *The New York Times,* February 13,1977.
   —Novak, Jeremiah; "Trilateralism: A New World System," *America,* February 5, 1977.

We are glad that the global economic system is discovering the limitations, even for business, of military rule and repression. Violating human rights does not work in the long run for the capitalist system.

As Christians we cannot take the human rights issue lightly. Human rights were born with Creation, when God made male and female in his own image. And human rights were made the core of the Gospel when God "became flesh"—like one of us. People were not made for the system, but the system for the people.

Human rights violations in Latin America during this decade are so painful and intolerable because they are taking place in a continent that considers itself Christian. Yes, there are violations of human rights all over the world, in 110 countries, in the Soviet Union and in the Arab and Muslim countries. But in Latin America they are not materialistic governments torturing Christians, nor Muslims repressing Christians, but Christians repressing and torturing Christians! And they are doing it in the name of anti-communism and for "Christian and Western civilization"!

When Diane Houstoun, Elizabeth Käsemann's friend, was detained, tortured and abused during interrogations, she discovered that one of her young interrogators carried a swastika cross and the other a Christian cross. "We are good Catholics," the latter told her. The recurrent anti-Semitism and traditional distorted Christianity were fused together in the same ballet of terror, denying human life and dignity.

"The cry of my people" is the cry for the recovery of the full humanizing Gospel of Jesus Christ.

—Novak, Jeremiah; "Outline of World Economic Action for Carter: How Trilateral World Aid Third World," *The Christian Science Monitor.*
—"Trilateralists at Top: New Foreign Policy Elite," *U.S. News and World Report,* February 21, 1977.
—See also *Monthly Review,* June-July-August 1977.
—Whitman, Marina, V.N.; "Carter's Trilateral 'Conspiracy,' *The Christian Science Monitor,* February 7, 1977.

5

WOMEN'S LIBERATION:
Latin American Style

When we speak of human rights we cannot leave aside women's rights because, as has been rightly said by the North American women's liberation movement, the oppression of women is the oldest oppression in the world. Friedrich Engels wrote, "The first oppression of classes was that of the feminine sex by the masculine." And his disciple August Bebel added, "Woman was a slave before slavery existed."[1]

What is the situation of women in Latin America and what is being done in the southern hemisphere for the cause of women's liberation?

The problem is as real in Latin America as in other parts of the world. Women suffer oppression and discrimination one way or another in all our countries. But the situation and the meaning of the struggle for women's rights differ from country to country, from one class or sector of society to another, inside the same country. We cannot make generalizations. Women from the South and from the North have some things in common, but there are also great differences in priorities and in the concept of liberation itself.

This fact came dramatically to the fore at the International Women's Year Conference, organized by the United Nations and held in Mexico City in 1975. The following story is that of Domitila Barrios de Chungara, a woman from the tin mines of Bolivia who participated in the Mexico City deliberations. She was a delegate to the Tribune, a conference of women representing nongovernmental organizations held at the same time as the UN conference, which only government representatives attended.

A Miner's Wife in the Tribune

In preparation for International Women's Year, a woman

filmmaker from Brazil was passing through Bolivia and, while trying to get in touch with different women in the country, interviewed and filmed Domitila Chungara in the desolate mining camp of Siglo XX. She was impressed with the Housekeepers Association in the mines and decided that Domitila should be heard in the world encounter. She promised her an invitation from the United Nations.

The invitation came and the miners' wives and the miners' union supported Domitila, sending her to represent their cause at the Tribune. Other Bolivian women were invited to participate in the UN conference on women, but Domitila was the only Bolivian woman invited to the Tribune. At the time she was the General Secretary of the *Asociacion de Amas de Casa* (Housekeepers Association) at the mines.

It wasn't easy for Domitila to leave Bolivia, which was experiencing one of its most repressive periods. Government agents had banned all labor unions, searched the miners' headquarters and destroyed their radio stations. The Ministry of Interior (a repressive apparatus of the government) was using stalling techniques to defer her visa. Finally, when the miners threatened to strike and to file a complaint with the United Nations, the government let her leave, warning her that if she made unfavorable comments on the Bolivian situation, she would not be allowed to return. She arrived in Mexico after the Tribunal had already started.

Let her recall her impressions of the event in her own style (which loses some of its original flavor when translated into English).

I had the idea that the Tribune would be people, people like me, with similar problems—peasant and women workers from all the world, oppressed and persecuted people. . . . It was my first experience and I imagined to listen to certain things that would make me progress in life, in the struggle, in my work, see?

Well, at that moment a *gringa* (American woman), with her blonde hair, and with things here around the neck, with her hands in the pockets, approached the microphone, and said to the assembly:

I have simply asked for the microphone to tell you my experience. To us, men should give us a thousand and one medals because we prostitutes have the courage to sleep with so many men.

'Bravo!' yelled several of them. And clapped.

Well, with my *compañera* (fellow-woman) we left the place, because there hundreds of prostitutes had met to deal with their problems. And we went to another building. There the lesbians were meeting. And, again, their discussion was that they feel happy and proud to love another woman . . . that they must fight for their rights. . . . .

Those weren't my interests. And for me it was incomprehensible that so much money was being spent to discuss such things at the Tribune. Because I had left my *compañero* (companion-husband) with seven children, having to work every day in the mine. I had left my country to make known my homeland, how it suffers, that in Bolivia the magna carta of the United Nations is not obeyed. I wanted to make known all this, to listen to what they said of the other exploited countries and of other groups that have been liberated. And to run into these kind of problems? . . . I felt somewhat lost.

In other halls, some women stepped up and said: man is the scourge. . . . Man is the one that creates wars, man is the one that creates nuclear weapons, man is the one who beats women. . . . so, what is the first fight to carry on to reach equal rights for women? First we have to make war to the male. If the male has 10 lovers, then, let the female have 10 lovers, too. If the male spends all his money in bars spreeing, let the female do the same. . . .

That was the mentality and concern of several groups, and for me it was a hard shock. We were speaking different languages, see? . . . And there was a lot of control of the microphone.

Then a group of Latin Americans joined together and we turned down all that. We made known our common problems, and what our human condition, and how most women live. We also said that, for us, the first and principal work was not to fight against our *compañeros* (companions) but with them to change the system for another one, where men and women may have the right of life, work and of our own organization.

But, as soon as reports and proposals were coming, the things began to change. For instance, those women were defending prostitution, birth control and all those things, wanting to impose them as primary problems to be discussed at the Tribune. For us those were real problems, but not the fundamental ones.

Let's Speak About Us . . . Women

In that kind of situation, communication was hardly possible and a clash was inevitable. Domitila Chungara says that she felt like a Cinderella, introducing herself as "a miner's wife from Bolivia," after so many women gave their degrees as lawyers, journalists or representing important organizations. She tells of a discussion with Betty Friedan, "the great feminist leader from the United States," whose "feminist statements" the Latin Americans dissented from because they left out their fundamental problems. Betty Friedan confronted the Latin American women, telling them that they were "manipulated by men," that they should give up their "belligerent activity," that they were thinking only about "politics" and ignoring totally the feminine issues, "as the Bolivian delegation is doing." Domitila stood up to answer, trying unsuccessfully to reach the floor, asking for the right of defense. Then the leader of a Mexican delegation approached Domitila, saying:

Let's speak about us, madam. . . We are women. Look madam, forget the massacres. We have spoken enough of that. We have heard you enough. Let's speak about us . . . of you and me . . . of women.

Domitila, who has a rude kind of eloquence, answered:

Okay, let's speak about us. But if you permit me, I will begin, madam. I have known you for a week. Every morning you arrive with a different dress; but not me. Every day you arrive with your make-up and your hairdo, as one who has time to spend in an elegant beauty parlor and who can spend money on that; but not me. I see that every evening a chauffeur is waiting for you in a car to take you home; but not me. And to present yourself as you do, I am sure you live in an elegant home, in an elegant residential area, huh? However, we, the miners' women, have only a small borrowed living place, and when our husband dies or gets sick or is retired from the company, we have 90 days to vacate the house, and we are on the street.

Now, my dear lady, tell me: Have you a similar situation to mine? Have I anything similar to your situation? Of what equality, then, are we going to speak about? We cannot, at this moment, be equals, even as women, don't you think so?

85

Another Mexican woman intervened in the conversation, saying to Domitila:

> Listen, what do you want? She is the leader of a Mexican delegation and she has preference. Besides, we have been here too benevolent to you, we have heard you by radio, TV, the press, and in the Tribune. I am tired of applauding you.

Domitila recalls her immediate reaction:

> It infuriated me for her to say such a thing, because it made me think that the problem I was stating served only to make me a theater character to be applauded. . . . I felt like if they were treating me as a clown.

> Listen, madam, I said. And who has asked your applause? If with applauses problems could be solved, my hands wouldn't be enough to applaud and I had not come from Bolivia to Mexico, leaving behind my children, to speak about our problems. Keep the applause for yourself, because I have received more beautiful applauses from the calloused hands of the miners.[2]

The exchange of words was harsh. The women's intentions may have been good, but they were speaking different languages and from different existential situations. They were not living in Domitila's world; they couldn't see Domitila's people's sufferings; they were not aware of Domitila's husband and other miners' situations, coughing up their lungs, spitting blood as a consequence of the mine sickness. They didn't see Domitila's undernourished children; they didn't know of Domitila's daily rising at 4 a.m. to supplement her husband's miserable salary and going back to sleep near midnight. How could they understand the mine women's leader, who had been organizing a parallel women's union to support the miners' union in their struggle for a few cents' increase in salary, or for a few cents less in basic food prices? A woman who—with other miners' wives—had marched, protested, cried, faced military squads, pleaded for their imprisoned husbands; a woman who gave birth to a dead baby in prison because of beating and torture; a woman who had been separated from her husband and her children and "exiled" inside her own country because of her commitment to justice and to her people. Yes, she was a woman: but that was all they had in common.

As Domitila concluded when they finally gave her the floor, "You, what can you know about all this? And, of course, for you the solution is to fight men. And that's all. But for us, that is not the principal solution."

Domitila Barrios de Chungara is a born fighter. She is one of five girls who lost their mother when still growing up. Her father did not have a son, but she incarnated his own sense of justice and commitment to the people. She is a feminist in her own way, not fighting for her own personal liberation but for the liberation of her people. She knows where the enemy is—not in her husband or in the other sex, but in a dehumanizing economic and social system. She made room for herself, a room not only at home but in public militancy, in spite of traditional prejudices about women's role. But she knows that men and women of her class have to work together for a common liberation, for a better world. She says:

> Because our position is not like the feminists. We consider that our liberation consists, first of all, in getting our country liberated from the imperialist yoke . . . and to reach conditions for a total liberation, also in our feminine condition. The important thing for us, is the participation for our companions, together with us. Only this way we will get better days, better people and more happiness for all.[3]

Domitila Chungara is sounding here the cry of many Latin American women—which is half of "the cry of my people."

Striking Women in Chile

Dorothee Sölle, a German liberation theologian who has a very clear position on women's liberation from a European perspective, had the opportunity to give second thought to her assumptions when she was accompanying the group of women in Chile who were in a hunger strike, demanding information about their abducted husbands, fathers, sons and brothers.

Dorothee Sölle is a woman and a liberationist, but she was aware of the limitations of her solidarity with other women struggling for liberation in Latin America. In writing of her experience in Chile she says:

> . . . I accepted the invitation with some doubts and reservations. What was the strike all about? The women whose cause I went to endorse slept on mattresses on the stone floors of churches—I stayed in a hotel. Pinned on their clothing were pictures of their husbands, sons and friends

who have disappeared—I came back to my family. Their fight includes physical suffering—I fight only with my typewriter and my voice. All of them were ready to "give their lives for the truth," as their slogan indicated, and they still risk the possibility that they themselves might disappear—I could, at most, be expelled *from* Chile or have minor troubles. In brief, they starve—I eat.

And yet, Dorothee Sölle was able to transcend those limitations to give what she had in solidarity: her typewriter and her voice. This is something that many of us have. Something which we can put at the service of the silenced and the voiceless struggling for human liberation.

One of the women lying on the floor of a church during the long hunger strike suddenly removed the picture of her son which was pinned on her dress and gave it to Dr. Sölle. He was only 26 at the time of his disappearance in 1974, a highly respected teacher at the Poid Institute, and a spokesman for the students. There is good reason for his mother to believe that he is dead. A brother-in-law who has close connections with the junta has told her, "Your son is dead and there are more than 1,000 others. Stop searching for him. It is useless." This mother was not crying. She said proudly, "He was and remained unbroken. He did not speak, he did not betray any names. None of his friends have been arrested."

The woman theologian from Germany described the condition of the women strikers: under medical supervision they drank three liters of boiled water per day (heated to avoid a cold) and took salt and vitamins. When she asked those women who they were, they would respond, "I am the mother of . . .," "the employee of . . .," "the daughter of . . . ." Dr. Sölle reflects:

> In the women's movement we have tried for a long time to overcome this kind of self-definition by relation to males, but here it makes sense in a very different way.

It makes sense. Husbands, children, fathers, friends are not unimportant in a woman's self-definition, even if that constellation of loved ones is not the only identity criteria. They represent love, and love *is* liberation. Because, in a Christian understanding, liberation is not only *from* but *for*. A liberation that does not help us to give ourselves to others is not Christian liberation. This is precisely part of the message that Dorothee Sölle received in Chile, while listening to a song in a Chilean coffeehouse:

Where is my son?" by Solōn.

To love with the face toward the sun without hiding
To love—every moment to give your life
To love—not to wear a mask, to show the face
To love—to take a risk for your people (at this point there
    was a great applause from the audience)
I cannot live without loving.

"It was this kind of love," says Mrs. Sölle, "the love willing to risk, that I saw in so many of the hunger strikers at the various churches." The visiting theologian was allowed to visit the penitentiary in Santiago where 31 political prisoners, despite their poor health, had joined the hunger strike to support the relatives of the abducted. She was deeply impressed by what she saw and by the mood of the people:

> In this damp, dark room, poorly heated with four small kerosene stoves, the mood among the prisoners and their visitors was incredible. I have never seen so much overt tenderness in a group: a silent, sad and encouraging affection was shared between male and female friends, husband and wife, mothers and sons.[4]

Might it be that "overt tenderness" in the midst of suffering and repression is an essential element of human liberation? Liberation for both—male and female.

"Four Women Confront a Nation"

Wilson T. Boots gave this title to the story of four miners' wives who triggered the most dramatic change in Bolivia in the last decade. He calls it "a miracle."[5] And it was. The powerful miracle of the powerless.

Immediately after Christmas 1977 four Bolivian miners' wives and their 14 children came from the mines to the city of La Paz to start a hunger strike. They were demanding the return and reinstatement of their husbands, who had been fired from the mines and expelled from the country, leaving their families behind in utter destitution. They were also supporting the demand of the churches and other groups for a general amnesty for the 20,000 Bolivian exiles who were not allowed to come back to their own country. This move was daring, because under the military regime no strikes were allowed, political parties had been abolished and unions had been prohibited. So they went to the Archbishop's headquarters to be protected from the police while keeping their hunger strike. Some people were upset because the children might die after a few days of fasting. "What's the difference?" said the miners' wives. "They will die in the mines anyway." (One of those mothers had already lost four of her children.) A group of Christians pleaded for the children and offered themselves to substitute for them. The mothers allowed their children to receive food, but they kept them with them during the strike.

The press was not giving much coverage. The Government ridiculed the strike through editorials and press releases. Every day a small group would join the hunger strike, taking refuge in a Catholic or a Methodist church or in universities in nine different cities of Bolivia, so that at any given moment there were 1,300 strikers. But two weeks passed without any visible result, and the first casualties were taken to hospitals in critical condition.

By invitation of the Human Rights Assembly, a three-person ecumenical committee representing the National Council of Churches of the U.S.A., the World Council of Churches and the U.S. Catholic Conference was sent out to Bolivia. They arrived just in time to see the Government retaliating. The authorities called a general strike to counteract the hunger strike. After midnight Government agents and the police searched the leading newspaper's headquarters and churches, and the strikers were violently taken to hospitals or to prisons.

It seemed that everything was over. Then the Archbishop of La Paz decided to take an extreme, unusual and dramatic measure: unless a solution was found, churches would remain closed that week and priestly services would not be provided except for the dying. Then negotiations were resumed, including the participation of the ecumenical visiting team. Finally after 21 days of the hunger strike, the Government gave up and proclaimed a general amnesty.

The unbelievable had happened. The miners' wives went back to the mines, knowing their husbands would return and be reinstated. In a few days politicians and unionists who had been in exile for six years were walking the streets of Bolivia's cities, participating in the process of "democratization" called for by the Government.

When asked, "Why did you start this hunger strike at Christmas time?" Nely de Paniagua, a miner's wife said, "Because this is the time we celebrate the birth of our Savior who came to bring justice and peace on earth." This woman never went to school—she had to learn to read by herself—but she knew what the Gospel was all about.

These brave Bolivian women of today are good heirs of the brave women who fought with their men for Bolivia during the independence wars. And they are Christians, practicing Christians, who were ready to pay the price of an incarnated Gospel of peace and justice. They were able to give an example, to risk their lives and the lives of their children when nobody dared to challenge the dominating powers—to challenge Christians and churches and finally to prevail over the apparently unconquerable power of a dictatorship that ruled the country with an iron hand, unchallenged for eight years. Today Bolivia is still enjoying the "democratic opening" which these daring women brought about in the beginning of 1978.

These women, like their sister, Domitila Chungara, are telling us that women's liberation is inseparable from the liberation of their people. When they were offered freedom, the return of their husbands and their jobs in the mines, they refused to stop the hunger strike unless the Government granted a total amnesty for all political prisoners and exiles. They were showing us that individual liberation, without liberation for others, is not real liberation and is not Christian. They were demonstrating, at great cost, that we are only truly liberated when we give ourselves for others' liberation.

The "cry of my people," coming through the Bolivian women, is a battle cry and a cry of hope.

Yes, Machismo Is Here

What about *machismo* in Latin America?

It is also true that there is such a thing as discrimination and oppression of women in Latin America. To overcome it is part of our struggle for human liberation.

The Spanish word *machismo* is used in English to describe the belief in male superiority or domination and its related behavior. *Machismo* comes from *macho,* male among animals. It has consequently some sexual connotations such as braggadocio, masculinity, domination, sexual potency. It is at the roots of sexual violence and crimes of passion. It is the source of romantic love, poetry, and erotica and the more innocent practice of *piropos,* saying nice things to girls and ladies passing in the street—a subtler and more poetic compliment than the whistling of American males!

But, as Dr. Antonia Ramirez of the Dominican Republic says, "*Machismo* is not only a biological phenomenon but more a socio-cultural one." It includes the idea that man has to be obeyed and served while woman is destined to a subservient role. He has the right to command, she has the obligation to obey, or perhaps the right to request. He has the last word at home and a monopoly of certain physical and economic activities. Women are for home, for children, and for certain more "feminine" professions (teaching, secretarial work, etc.). It also includes the idea that there is a double standard of behavior, one for males, another for females. To the question, "Is infidelity to be condemned more in a woman than in a man?" asked in a nation-wide sampling done in the Dominican Republic, 71.3 percent of the males said "yes."[6]

Machismo is strong among Latin peoples. We inherited it from the Spanish and the Portuguese. But in Indian pre-Columbian civilizations women were also under male domination—those were patriarchal societies as well. It is said that Latin peoples have a Mediterranean heritage in relation to women which is common to Muslims, Jews and Christians, with some very old characteristics: the sacralization of feminine virtue, the cloistering of women and the killing of the adulterous woman. This code for women has older roots in the endogamic ideal of Mediterranean tribes, among whom women are treated as private property, as minors and as beings deprived of reason.[7]

A universally known branch from this traditional tree is the famous figure of *Don Juan,* the irresistible male who goes from one female conquest to another. This literary figure—with so many imitators in real life—is frankly in retreat, after the psychological diagnosis that he is an insecure, frightened man, pathetically trying to demonstrate to himself his masculinity, unable to enjoy love and women. And yet there is still in Latin America today the deeply rooted idea that man has to demonstrate his masculinity, his virility by the number of his sexual conquests, showing off as a sort of "dormitory champion." The Latin American movies have popularized some other types, direct descendants of Don Juan: the Argentine *macho,* the bohemian of the *taongs* who adores his mother, who idealizes "the good girl" and who blames the "bad woman" for his lot. Most of the themes of the *tangos* are about betrayal or the ungrateful woman who forgets her good man to marry a rich guy or who runs off with an adventurer. Or the Mexican gentleman, the *charro,* the brave and handsome rancher, good to his friends and generous with his workers, irresistible to awed *campesino* (peasant) girls. Or his urban cousin, the poor author struggling to reach fame while his girl prefers the millionaire. . . .

This sexual and sentimental *machismo* is ambivalent in its manifestations: on one hand, the idealization and worship of women in poetry, in romance, in gallantry, in veneration of mothers and in worship of the Virgin Mary. But on the other hand, there is the subjugation of women at home and the discrimination against women in public life and society.

The Bolivian anthropologist Mario Montano suggests that male and female values and attitudes have to do with the type of culture and society, observing that while in the highlands of the Altiplano and the valleys men are discreet and subdued in their behavior, women are towering and arrogant. In the plains and lowlands it is the opposite: man is boastful and dominating and women are subdued and passive. To complicate the picture, the *chola* woman of the cities (the Indian-white *mestiza*) is strong, self-sufficient, smart and active in business, while men are peripheral to her life. The *chola* clearly shows the characteristics of a matriarchal style of life. According to Montaño, in the first case we have the characteristics of an agricultural society (including the worship of land's fertility), and in the second case we have the traits of a cattle-raising culture:

> In what can be called the "horse culture" is where the *machista* attitude is predominantly developed, where women become an instrument of pleasure . . . or the object of bad treatment. It would be enough to analyze the life of the Arabs in the desert, the North American *cowboy,* the Mexican *charro,* the *llanero,* the man of the plains of Colombia and Venezuela, the Argentine *gaucho,* or the Chilean *guaso,* which are different versions of our *camba* from the Bolivian plains.[8]

Institutionalized Machismo

But *machismo* is more than a folkloric remembrance from the time of our ancestors. It is alive and well—and institutionalized—in the structures and practices of our urban societies: in differences in education, in compensation for work, in participation at the executive level of industry and commerce, or in the political decision-making of our countries.

Consider a few statistics from Latin American countries. In Brazil only 20 percent of remunerated workers are women, and their salaries are below those of men for the same type of work. In Argentina, 23 percent of the workers are women. In Venezuela nearly 20 percent of the economically active population are women; they have a tendency to disappear after the age of 35, when they have qualifications which permit them to aspire to higher positions. In Salvador 26 percent of the agricultural workers are women; in industry they work up to 14 hours a day to earn one-fourth of what men receive for the same workday. In several countries, however, law requires the payment of equal salary for equal work.

As for education, women are the bulk of the illiterate masses of Latin America: 40 percent in total, with percentages going as high as 68 percent illiteracy among women in Guatemala, 70 percent in Bolivia, 85 percent in Haiti. In some rural areas, in Bolivia and elsewhere, educating girls is considered a waste of time and money although this is changing with the increase of public schools and opportunities. Statistics show that in Bolivia, more girls drop out of school. It is a surprising fact, however, that in high school there are more girls than boys. This is also true in Uruguay, but in the Dominican Republic only 1.1 percent are women. At university level in most countries women are between 20 percent and 25 percent of the students registered, but they have higher percentages in some departments, such as humanities, education and social work.

Machismo also exists in the church, a fact that became clear in the Puebla Conference of Catholic Bishops, the top assembly of a church with an all-male priesthood, totally controlled by men, where women's concerns had to be voiced by an outside group, "Women for Dialogue." Among Protestant churches it is becoming more common to have women ministers, but there is still a lot to be done in church structures and even more in the inner mental structures of members, including those of women themselves. It is a common occurrence in church meetings for women not to vote for women as delegates to assemblies or committees!

Women in Politics

In all Latin American countries women have the right to vote. They have had the right in Brazil, Cuba and Uruguay since 1934; in Venezuela since 1945; in Mexico since 1953, and in Honduras since 1955. In some countries women's participation in elections (when we have them!) becomes the decisive factor, and politicians are beginning to pay attention to women's concerns and to the utilization of women's preferences and prejudices in electoral propaganda. In Nicaragua, Violeta Chamorro, the widow of the journalist assassinated by the Somoza regime, is one of the five-member ruling junta. It is common in most of our countries to have women in Congress and the Senate. In Bolivia a woman, Linda Gueiler, was elected chairperson of the House, and she became the President of the country after the last political crisis in November, 1979, with three more women in her cabinet. Argentina had a woman president for two years. Often, however, they are just "token" figures, not reflecting the fact that half of the voting population are women.

In Chile, under the Marxist-oriented government of President Allende, women were very active in civic, social, economic and political activities. In Uruguay, during the days of the *Frente Amplio* (Wide Coalition), the last try for a democratic transition, women participated in unprecedented ways in political campaigns.

In Cuba—as can be expected in a socialist country where women are considered a basic asset to production and to society in general—the education and participation of women has increased considerably during these years. The Cuban Federation of Women was born in 1960, and it now has 1,600,000 members (one-fifth of the total population). The literacy campaign, which eliminated illiteracy on the island, reached half a million women. Ninety thousand other women who left school early in life have obtained the sixth grade certificate. Women's registration in secondary schools has reached 56 percent of the total enrollment; in pre-university, 57 percent; in teachers' schools, 67 percent; and in art schools, 62 percent. The number of women engaged in remunerated work grew from one-quarter of a million in 1968 to one-half million four years later—almost 50 percent of the total work force. Most women work in light industry, public health and education. Prostitutes were given the opportunity to learn other trades and professions, and prostitution has practically disappeared from the island. The Cubans seem to share Mao Tse-tung's conviction that "without women's liberation there will be no revolution."

Changes Are Coming

Changes are coming, however. In almost every Latin American country legislation is recognizing juridical equality for women. Present Bolivian legislation is typical: women have equal rights, freedoms and guarantees recognized by the constitution. A married woman acquires her husband's nationality without losing her own. She can adopt and keep her husband's name but may also keep her own name. Wives have equal rights and duties in the conduct and management of the marriage contract as well as in the rearing and educating of children. They are free to work in their own profession. A couple's income is considered communal, to be divided into equal parts if the marriage is dissolved. In cases of divorce the decision of child custody is not decided in terms of sex. The single mother has the right to demand a paternity investigation and material and moral support.

Abortion laws, however, are very rigid, with severe penalties for both the mother and the performer of the abortion. The laws have grave consequences, resulting in clandestine and unsafe abortions with a high death rate. The Roman Catholic stance on abortion has influenced this type of legislation all over Latin America.

So the problem of discrimination against women is not so much a matter of legislation as of practice. Laws can be changed more easily than mental attitudes, and inveterate habits—particularly those of women themselves. As José B. Adolph says, "To overthrow a government is easier than to make a prejudice disappear." This is particularly true in Latin America, where we have overthrown so many governments but where prejudice is not lacking!

The Other Side of the Coin: "The Manipulated Man"

Nobody has gone so far, we believe, in blaming women for present conditions as the Argentine sociologist Esther Vilar, who wrote the famous bestseller translated into several languages, *The Manipulated Man*.*

Her thesis is that the problem today is not the oppressed woman but the tame male, the domesticated man. Man may believe that *he* is oppressing *her,* but no woman is forced to submit to the will of man nowadays. On the contrary; all possibilities for the independence of women have been recognized today. If they have not got rid of the yoke, it is because the yoke does not exist. On the other hand, the male has become accustomed to his servitude. He does not want to be free, and he even finds his pleasure in unfreedom. Or, at least, he doesn't suspect that his situation could be different!

What is this servitude all about? Esther Vilar puts it bluntly: Man is a human being that works—and he works for woman because, by definition, a woman is a human being that does not work, who lives by the work of man. This happens throughout the wide spectrum of society: to the man who goes to work in his limousine, the one who goes in a second-hand car, or the one who takes a bus to his workshop:

> In whatever work he may do, writing figures in columns, treating patients, driving a bus, managing an enterprise, the male is constantly part of a gigantic merciless system, ready for the exclusive purpose of his maximum exploitation; and until death he is condemned to this system.

> No, it cannot be believed that males do all these things by pleasure, without feeling ever the wish to change trade. They

---

* English edition published by Bantam Books, 1974.

97

do it because they have been tamed, domesticated, trained for it: all their life is a sad succession of mimicries of a domesticated animal. The male that stops dominating the game, who starts earning less money, is "a failure" and loses everything: wife, family, house, even the meaning of life . . . even a hiding place for his soul in the world.

While we listen to this tirade, questions pile up. What about the unending chain of domestic work for women—raising children, keeping the house, handling the family finances, etc.? What about working and professional women and those women who have to work both at home and outside? What about the new generation of women students, preparing for a career and opting for a companionship type of relationship with males? The Argentine sociologist has her answers to those questions. Let's summarize them.

As to domestic chores, today any housekeeping can be finished in two hours, thanks to the automatic appliances invented by men for women. But women spend a lot of time in baking cakes or biscuits, ironing, sewing, washing windows and spending their free time on themselves, putting rollers in their hair, painting their nails, etc. What they call their "domestic work" is their entertainment, their "feminine vices." They are not interested in spending their saved time in reading, in learning, because they have lost their curiosity, their spiritual interests.

Since the age of 12 they have become geared toward getting a male who would support them for the rest of their lives. Publications for women show the intellectual level of their readers: they don't care about anything unless it comes with the "feminine" subject or label. Women are not interested in anything but themselves. When men appear in those feminine magazines it is only as an object, with instructions about how to get him hooked or how to keep him.

As to children, they are only instruments for realizing the woman's purpose (they are also a justification for man and his submission to the woman). Certainly there are some discomforts during pregnancy, delivery and a little after, but that is a low price to pay for a guarantee of comfort and irresponsibility for the rest of her life. As soon as children go to nurseries and schools, the woman is free again to do what she wants. Children are used as "hostages," to justify her exploitation of the male in the name of motherhood and children. Mothers are not interested in children *per se,* as can be seen by the fact that they care only for their own and not other people's children. It is with children that the domestication of the male—and the training of the girl for her future exploitation of the male—begins. Mothers begin the taming of the male, preparing the boy to be eternally grateful for his mother's "sacrifices" and to serve women.

Yes, it is true—continues Esther Vilar—that women are crowding the universities today and that thousands of them are working in offices and factories. But those places are just the hunting ground for the exploited male. Those from well-to-do families go to good universities where they can find males who eventually will earn for them at least as much as their fathers. Girls from families of lower income will work in a factory, a store, an office, a hospital, *provisionally*, with the same purpose. "Offices, factories and universities are not, for women, anything else than gigantic marriage agencies." Study and work last only until the wedding ceremony or, at most, till the first pregnancy. Then the woman will pretend that she left work and study for love of the man she has chosen.

The Total Woman

According to Esther Vilar, author of this controversial bestseller on the manipulated man, women have developed a series of techniques and operations for taming the male. The taming of animals is done with a stick and sugar. The human male—since childhood—becomes easily addicted to the sugar of *praise,* and he will do anything to be praised. To promote self-confidence in the male, the woman resorts to another trick: *self-humiliation.* She will pretend to be weaker, less intelligent and less able than men. Further, *sex* is another link in the chain of the tame male. "Sex is, of course, a pleasure to women, but not the major one. . . . It is down below in her scale of values, compared with, let's say, a cocktail party or buying a pair of glossy pumpkin colored boots." Women administer sex in line with their purpose of male subservience. Vilar even ventures the hypothesis that women use the church and the clerical "lobby" in their favor, with the notions of "good and evil" and constant defense of women and men's responsibility towards them.

Praise of males, female self-humiliation, the sex game. . . . Aren't these Marabel Morgan's prescriptions for *the total woman* (in her book *The Total Woman,* published by Revell)?

Finally, the male does his part in taming himself through idealizing the woman and through the powerful effect of the publicity industry. Market research tells men what women wish and their wishes are stimulated through the media. The woman is the client and the man is the seller. But the gun backfires: the woman praises the man for working for her; the man praises the woman so she can spend all the money he has earned. Man is a prisoner of his own trap. And the American man is "the most successfully manipulated male on earth."

Of course, this generalization of an innocent tame male and a villainous woman exploiting him is unacceptable. But there is enough of a grain of truth in what she says to complete the picture of male-female relationships in our societies today. It is a fact that males and females are both victims and victimizers in the same system. What Esther Vilar says about "women" in general can be applied to an important sector of society, even though it cannot be applied in the same way to the poor women of our oppressed Latin American masses. And, besides, it is not true of many professional and working women who are independent, or of those who are struggling to survive and to support a family on their own. Esther Vilar clearly has in mind affluent women of the suburban "villas," those who pefer that style of life. Women who have the so-called "Señora complex."

Esther Vilar's opinion of women's liberation is not very positive, either. True, there are reasons for this struggle, but the intellectual leaders of the movement have missed the mark. Women's liberation has failed:

> It is sad and grotesque at the same time that women of the Women's Lib in North America—who really have certain motives to fight—have dilapidated all their power, all their publicity, all their time and work, combating against who is not their enemy. It is sad and grotesque how they harass with a constant defamation their own possible allies—the males—while they spoil with excessive praise the true culprit of the dilemma in which they are (the exploiter woman). Not one single male has expressed against them. . . . And men are paying for the defeat. . . . And women have not come of age either. Because the true liberation of women would be to liberate them of their privileges. . . .

Esther Vilar does not give guidelines for solutions. She sounds rather pessimistic, dedicating her book to "the person not appearing in it: the few men who do not allow themselves to be domesticated and to the few women who are not salable."

Let us conclude that, on one hand, the oppression of women and their liberation depend on their social class. And on the other hand, that there is no solution in either case without a common participation of men and women for a better society for both. We liberate together or we will not be liberated.

6

THE CHURCH DISCOVERS THE POOR ... AND THE GOSPEL

Mission in the '80s

The major fact of the Christian church in Latin America in the last third of the twentieth century has been no less than the discovery of the poor and, consequently, the rediscovery of the Gospel!

Probably Latin America is the continent in the world where the church still is, and is called to be, a decisive factor in the life and destiny of peoples. When Pope John Paul II came to Mexico in February 1979 to inaugurate the episcopal conference of the region, 3,000 reporters came from all over the world and millions of people thronged the streets. Where else in the world could a regional episcopal conference attract such world attention or such an audience? *Not only* the church and Christians all over Latin America were on their tiptoes waiting for the final outcome of the Puebla Conference of Bishops in Mexico. The governments, students, workers and peasants of the whole continent, as well, awaited the news. Such expectations can only be explained by the role the church has been playing during the last few years, since Medellín in 1968. The Protestant churches cannot match this record nor can their influence compare at all with that of the Catholic Church—of an essential character—but their role and influence in relation to both the Catholic Church and the Latin American people is by no means negligible.

The Protestant Churches Discover Society

As we have said before, one of the strong points of the Protestant version of Christianity is its emphasis on the individual, both in the personal experience of Christ and the ethical demands on the

101

individual. We Protestants were strong in the understanding of personal inner life, personal sins and personal virtues, but we were at a loss concerning social problems. We had no idea of the structural character of society or of its problems and dynamics. We could not grasp social problems except from an individualistic perspective. And we easily took refuge in the old evangelical half-truth: there will be no new society without new persons; the change of heart by conversion is the best guarantee of changing the world. But the historical realities of Latin America would not let us close our eyes or protect ourselves inside the shell of that pious refuge. Sooner or later, Protestants of a second and third generation had to discover society. But to face it we needed new disciplinary tools from both the social sciences and contemporary ideologies—including Marxism of one sort or another. We also needed a new understanding of the Gospel and a new theology.

In the early '60s a qualified sector of the Protestant leadership, from the historical churches and ecumenical groups, began to take anxious note of the Latin American context of the mission of the church and called the churches to "an incarnation in the sufferings and hopes of the society in which they live." The second Latin American Evangelical Conference (the most inclusive ecumenical assembly in Latin America, known as CELA), met in Huampani, Peru, in 1961. Throughout all the commissions and documents there was a clear call to the churches to overcome traditional spiritualistic individualism and to assume responsibilities in the dramatic situation of the Latin American continent, marked by population explosion, malnutrition, infant mortality, illiteracy, poverty, exploitation, rising expectations of the masses. The second CELA in 1961 was no longer justifying its presence in Latin America—as did the first one in Buenos Aires in 1949—but was concerned with Latin American society. There was joy, indeed, in the fact of unprecedented growth of the evangelical community in Latin America, but the churches were no longer satisfied merely with a narcissistic celebration or an introverted perspective of the church.

This discovery of society as the "correlate" of the church's mission was clear at the third CELA in Buenos Aires in 1969, where Protestants from all over the continent met under the theme "Debtors to the World." According to Orlando Costas, writing in his doctoral dissertation on Latin American missiological trends in recent years, Protestantism at the third CELA revealed a new consciousness, a new vision of social reality, a new critical awareness of the role of the church in society and a new incarnational theology of mission.[1]

This theology is grounded in the Incarnation of Christ, who identified himself with humanity in its misery in order to reconcile it with God, to bring power and the hope of a new life.[2] Of course, this new consciousness was not a homogeneous one among evangelical churches in Latin America. A new controversy was coming up, no longer on confessional or doctrinal issues but on ideological ones, precisely on the question of church and the world.

Manifesto to the Nation

The Protestant churches felt called to reassess their understanding of the Gospel and their own self-understanding in relation to society. "The most notable example among the churches is that of the Evangelical Methodist Church in Bolivia," says Oriando Costas, pointing to its "Manifesto to the Bolivian Nation" as "a landmark" in missiological thinking. The manifesto was issued by the church before Easter 1970 as a sort of "social creed," an introduction card to Bolivia's society when the EMCB became autonomous. It was read to the President of the Republic and the Commander-in-Chief of the armed forces and published in full in the Bolivian press. Later on it was translated into other languages and circulated around the world.[3] In the manifesto, the church defines itself as a Christian, Protestant, Methodist, Bolivian church; explains its *raison d'être* in the Gospel and Christian mission; analyzes and interprets the present Bolivian reality; and commits itself to work with other Christians and the Bolivian people for a new man and a new society. This is how the church sees itself in relation to society.

> Before all else our loyalty is to Jesus Christ and to the Gospel. A whole gospel which is "for all people and for all of humanity." Consequently, our loyalty is also to each person, and specifically to the Bolivian in our case, to whom this liberating gospel is directed, and whom we wish to serve in the name of Christ. . . .
>
> Our reason for existing is found in the Gospel of Jesus Christ, which implies the full humanization of humanity, the carrying out of God's purpose for the people he has created and redeemed. It has to do with a liberation, a salvation, which extends to all aspects of a person: the soul, the eternal destiny and also the historical, material, individual and social being. God is interested in all of life and not only in one part of it. This is the message of the Bible which we proclaim and desire to incarnate. . . .

Not only are there dehumanizing tendencies within people, there are dehumanizing forces encrusted in society. Sin also has a social and objective dimension. The social, political, cultural or economic structures become dehumanizing when they aren't at the service of "all persons and the whole person," in one word, when they become structures which perpetuate injustice. Structures are a product of persons but they assume an impersonal and even demonic character by going beyond the possibilities of individual action. Collective and concerted action to change said structures is necessary, for there is no structure which is sacred or unchangeable.

The God whom we know in the Bible is a liberating God, a God who destroys myths and alienations. A God who intervenes in history in order to break down the structures of injustice and who raises up prophets in order to point out the way of justice and mercy. He is the God who liberates slaves (Exodus), who causes empires to fall and who raises up the oppressed (Magnificat, Luke 1:52). This is the message of liberation and hope of the Gospel: "The Spirit of the Lord is upon me, because he has anointed me . . . to liberate the oppressed" (Luke 4:18-19). We are indebted to this message if we do not want to be found unworthy of our mission and our name.

The Christian Church cannot ally itself with any force which oppresses or dehumanizes the human person.

The EMCB was taking heed of "the cry of my people" and defining its mission in terms of a response to that cry. Other churches in Latin America were trying to respond in a similar way.

Ecumenical Groups Lead the Way

It is only fair to say that it was the emergence of Christian reflection and action groups that helped the churches to become aware of the challenges of Latin American society and to articulate their response to it. This is particularly true of the so-called "para-ecclesiastical" ecumenical groups such as Latin American Union of Youth (ULAJE), Latin American Evangelical Commission of Christian Education (CELADEC), the Student Christian Movement (MEC), Church and Society in Latin America (ISAL) and Urban Mission (MISUR). Another important one was the Commission for Evangelical Union in

Latin America (UNELAM), a sort of conciliar organ for evangelical ecumenism formed by some national councils and individual affiliated churches.

Orlando Costas considers ISAL "the most consistently radical Protestant ecumenical organization in Latin America." It has also been the most influential and, at the same time, the most controversial one among the churches.

ISAL began in Huampani, Peru in 1961, holding its first assembly just a week before the second CELA. The influence of its Bible studies, with their social analysis and concerns, was already apparent in the Latin American Evangelical Conference documents. In El Tabo, Chile, in 1965 ISAL was sharpening its analysis of Latin American society and discovering how the crisis was affecting society and the church itself. It was also the beginning of a new theological reflection, under the influence of the American theologian Richard Shaull and his revolutionary theology of history.

Meanwhile, ISAL publications, especially the quarterly *Cristianismo y Sociedad* (Christianity and Society), were providing the churches—or at least the concerned elite of the churches—with up-to-date information about Latin America, new tools of socioeconomic and political analysis, and some new biblical and theological insights. Several books were produced on the social responsibility of Christians, the relationship between faith and ideology, between Christianity and revolution and, finally, on the sweeping concept of liberation.

When the fourth ISAL Assembly met in Ñaña, Peru, in July 1971, the Christian elite was ready to become a movement or at least to encourage its members to participate in political, social, economic or ideological movements aiming at the transformation of Latin American society. By this time ISAL was no longer a purely Protestant ecumenical movement. It included a considerable and qualified number of Catholic priests, nuns and laypersons who were very active in several countries as well as union leaders and activists who were not formal members of any Christian church. An unprecedented ecumenical laboratory was under way, and ISAL became for many the sign of the new emerging church frontier with the world. Actually many Christian rebels found in ISAL their real ecclesial community, sharing with others a common commitment to a new person and a new society in the name of Christ. The publication *PASOS,* edited in Santiago de Chile by the theologian Hugo Assmann—a Catholic priest with a vast international experience—represented a new way of doing Christian theology: becoming a dynamic and dialectic process of action-reflection. The leadership of ISAL, together with radicalized priests from the Roman Catholic Church, became the original nucleus of the movement *Christians for Socialism,* a short-lived movement which had significant international repercussions.[4]

As could be expected, this process of growing engagement with society and of increasing radicalization was alienating the traditional sectors of the churches, both Catholic and Protestant. When the military coup overthrew the Allende government in Chile in 1973, repression was common in many other neighboring countries, the leadership of ISAL was scattered all over Latin America, and its structure was dismantled. Despite the fact—and the resistance to and criticism of ISAL ideas and commitments—the movement had a definite fertilizing effect in many thinking and concerned sectors of the churches all over Latin America. ISAL is dead now as an organization, but the churches will never be the same. ISAL has been "a catalyst and a ferment," according to Beatriz Melano Couch, an Argentine theologian. We may be perplexed, polarized, more or less engaged in society, but we cannot remain innocent any longer.

A similar process has been the one the Latin American Evangelical Commission for Christian Education (CELADEC) has experimented with. It began 30 years ago with a venture unique in the whole Christian world: the preparation and publication of a full Christian Education curriculum at an ecumenical level for the 20 Spanish-speaking republics. In the '60s it produced a popular Christian curriculum called *The New Life in Christ Course,* which started with the real situation of the common people of our countries. It was revolutionary in its perspective (salvation-history), in its content (the Bible and the real lives of people in dynamic relationship), and its methodology ("congregational encounters" rather than "lessons"; "experiences of immersion" rather than academic "teaching"). But the *New Life in Christ Course* itself was revolutionized in the process! Beginning with strong emphasis on the personal experience of the believer and the interpersonal relationships of the Christian, it moves on to the communitarian dimension of the faith, namely the church; then the last units in the third year of the course deal with society and the world. Not only did the subject change its focus at this third level, but the times had changed when the units were published. The new insights of the Brazilian pedagogue Paulo Freire—especially his concept of *conscientizacion*— were current among the avant-garde churches, and there was a new awareness of the structures and problems of Latin American society. Orlando Costas pointed out after reviewing the course that, while at first level the accent was on *spontaneous personal service* as the Christian's responsibility toward society, in the third level the stress fell on *planned social action.*

"Radical Evangelicals" and Pentecostals

So the Protestant churches, in many ways and at all levels, were discovering Latin American society and rediscovering new dimensions and new meanings of the Gospel. This was true even of the so-called conservative churches, the ones called "Evangelicals" in the United States. Latin American evangelicals have produced a new generation of leaders of an international caliber who cannot be labeled with the old cliches about "fundamentalists," "conservatives" or "evangelicals." Among them are such theologically articulate and sociologically enlightened leaders as Pedro Arana of Peru, from the Intervarsity movement (a member of the Peruvian Constituent Asssembly at the time of this writing); Orlando Costas, the first Latin American Protestant missiologist; Samuel Escobar, former editor of the university students' magazine *Certeza;* and René Padilla from Ecuador, who was recently a visiting professor at Union Theological Seminary in New York. The last two men had a decisive influence at the International Congress of World Evangelization at Lausanne, Switzerland, in 1974, stirring up the waters in the world evangelical encounter and moving the Congress ahead to reaffirm a whole Gospel, including social responsibility.

These new Latin American evangelicals (they probably would prefer to be called "radical evangelicals") would not let the Gospel be co-opted by conservative political forces or the adjective "evangelical" be monopolized by the conservative cultural Christianity represented by many so-called "evangelical missions" from North America.[5]

The same is true of many Pentecostals in Latin America today. Christian Lalive d'Epinay, after studying the Pentecostal movements in Chile, could describe them as living in a permanent state of "social strike," separated from the world and the social struggles of their neighbors and co-workers. But that description does not fit all Pentecostal groups in Latin America. Juan Carlos Ortiz, the leader of a charismatic renewal movement in Argentina, does not accept the separation between "spiritual" gospel or a "social" gospel but affirms just one gospel—spiritual, social and material. Manuel de Mello in Brazil would speak of "a gospel with bread," implying by bread, education, food, human dignity, liberation. The Venezuelan Pentecostals in their convening letter of San Cristobal said:

107

Looking at the great need of our peoples to come near to Bolivar's ideals (the union of these countries in freedom), our aim is to contribute to Christian solutions for the social, political, and economic problems of marginalized classes. . . .

We have seen throughout the years the pain of our marginalized brethren, while the Church which is their defense remains with hands tied up and empty faith unable to help except to die in a nauseating bed of conformism. . . .

Whereas social injustice has subjugated permanently the marginalized classes, we believe that the people of God must feel shame because of its attitude of indifference and should respond to the challenge Christ puts before us in this critical hour for humanity. . . .

These are Christian people coming from the marginalized poor masses of our society who had found new life and hope in Christ but who share and represent as well "the cry of my people," the dispossessed of Latin America. They have found Christ and they have discovered their people.

Medellín: The Church Discovers the Poor

By far the most dramatic change of the last decade or so has taken place in the Roman Catholic Church. The Second General Conference of Latin American Bishops in Medellín, Colombia, in 1968 has become a landmark for the church and for the recent history of Latin America. It has been called one of the most important events in the history of Latin American Christianity.

Why is this so?

Medellín was the end of an old era and the beginning of a new one. It was designated to update the Latin American Roman Catholic Church, putting it in line with Vatican II, but it went far beyond the Roman Council.

The theme was "Latin America in the Light of Vatican II" but in fact it was reversed to "The Vatican II in the light of Latin America"!

It would seem as if the old Roman Catholic Church of the Counter-Reformation suddenly was trying to catch up with a four-centuries-delayed Reformation and to get involved with the twentieth century revolution at the same time! The new era of the church was dramatized both by the personal presence of Pope Paul VI and the presence for the first time in history of representatives of non-Catholic churches. As we have already noted, there was in Medellín a new missionary outlook: official representatives of the Roman Catholic Church saw Latin America for the first time as "a world still unevangelized, a young continent remaining un-Christianized."[6]

At Medellín the Latin American Catholic Church reached a consciousness of its own identity (not merely as an outlet of the Roman curia) and started a quest for its own autochthonous pastoral orientation.[7] The church discovered a new way to be a "Latin American incarnation," not so much in its institutionalized forms as in the life and struggles of the people. And in doing so, it gave birth and thrust to what would later on be called the "theology of liberation."

But probably, the essential and revolutionary meaning of Medellín was the church's discovery of the poor and with it the recovery of the full biblical Gospel. The amazing and dominating factor in the preparatory process and in the Medellín Conference dynamics was the new awareness of the Latin American context and its implication for the church's mission. Never before in this continent had the church taken so seriously human and social conditions.

Latin American realities—some of which we have been in touch with in earlier chapters of this book—were imposing themselves on the bishops, priests, nuns and Christian laypersons all over the continent and coming to the fore in congresses, conferences, symposiums, public declarations, and on-the-march documents. The Medellín preparatory document describes these realities as a "struggle for development" and "a state of underdevelopment." The working draft concludes, "The challenge is not between status-quo and change; it is between violent change and peaceful change."

The 156 bishops were not alone in Medellín: there were 100 *periti* (experts) with them. With the help of Christian economists, sociologists and theologians, the bishops were able to see deeper than any impressionistic view of Latin American ills and to detect roots, causes, and underlying structures of injustice and oppression. They called those realities and structures "external colonialism," "money imperialism" and "internal colonialism." And they prophetically pointed to them as "institutionalized violence," as "a sinful situation."

The Temptation to Violence

It was 1968, a year of violence. Revolution was in the air. It was the year of the students' revolutions in Paris, Berkeley and Tokyo. It was the critical period of guerrilla warfare in several Latin American countries. Just two years before the Conference of Bishops, a Colombian priest, Camilo Torres, had died as a member of a guerrilla group in the jungles of his country. Exactly one year before that, Ernesto "Che" Guevara had been killed by the counter-insurgent forces of Bolivia, trained by the Pentagon. So revolutionary violence was a living issue for many Christians in Latin America. The bishops at Medellín could not avoid the issue.

But the bishops knew that revolutionary violence is not the root of the problem of our societies: it is only a symptom. Dom Helder Camara championed around the world a drastic but nonviolent revolution of the structures of injustice and oppression; at the same time he was very clear about the contemporary problem of violence. "There are three kinds of violence," he used to say. Violence No. 1 is the *institutionalized violence* of the system, which is producing poverty, suffering, marginalization, injustice. People react against Violence No. 1 with Violence No. 2: *revolutionary violence.* Then the governments and dominant classes respond to Violence No. 2 with Violence No. 3: *repressive violence,* fascistic violence. So violent revolution in Latin America is both fair and impossible. It is fair because it is a reaction against injustice and oppression. But it is impossible because of the terrifying power of the state to repress any revolution. Armies and police forces are trained and armed to repress successfully any revolutionary action.[8] So the bishops at Medellín denounced the true nature of violence encrusted in our societies:

> Many parts of Latin America are experiencing a situation of injustice which can be called institutionalized violence. The structures of industry and agriculture, of the national and the international economy, the cultural and political life all violate fundamental rights. Entire peoples lack the bare necessities and live in a condition of such dependency that they can exercise neither initiative nor responsibility. Similarly, they lack all possibility of cultural improvement and of participation in social and political life. Such situations call for a global, daring, urgent, and basically renewing change. It should surprise nobody that the *temptation to violence* should manifest itself in Latin America. It is wrong to abuse the patience of people who have endured for years a situation that would be intolerable if they were more aware of their rights as human beings.[9]

In fact, the fathers were saying peace is the work of justice; injustice is the root of violence.

In speaking this way in Medellín they were sensitively listening to "the cry of my people," oppressed by violence and tempted to violence.

Between Medellín and Puebla: The Price of Prophecy

The bishops spoke at Medellín with one voice. But it was not easy for many of them to speak out so clearly and prophetically back home. Some of them were not even really convinced of the new theological insights and the new stance of the church confronting the ruling powers. They had to face protest by the conservative constituency of the church and the reaction of repressive regimes and governments accustomed to using the church ideologically to support the system. Many theologians and activist groups were carrying the Medellín guidelines to "their last consequence." Many bishops became frightened and backed out.

An Argentine exile who was present with other Latin American exiles at a press conference in Puebla in 1979 gave this earnest testimony about Medellín:

> At the time of Medellín, I was 16 years old. Medellín gave to young people reasons to live, reasons to hope, above all it helped us to see that Christ had identified himself with the poor. We formed small prayer and reflection groups, and we began to see the necessity of living and working with the poor. This, for me, was a true conversion, in the sense that all the plans I had for my life were called into question when I realized how serious the needs of the poor were.

> But when we began to act on our convictions, the military became suspicious of us. As a result, many of us were arrested and imprisoned. Others had to go into exile. So when we learned that the bishops were going to meet again, in Puebla, we came here to ask for their support, to ask them to remember that we began because of what they said at Medellín. . . . We are children of Medellín.[10]

The "Children of Medellín" soon discovered the cost of prophecy. Repression hit the church head on. The French publication *Diffusion de L'information sur L'Amerique Latine* (D.I.A.L.) compiled around 1,500 names of priests, friars, bishops, nuns, and active laypersons who had been arrested, interrogated, defamed, tortured, kidnapped, assassinated or exiled during the decade 1968-1978. Among them 71 were tortured, 69 assassinated and 279 exiled (mostly foreign missionary priests and members of religious orders). The Latin American church became again "the church of the catacombs." This is the price of prophecy.

It is not by chance that the most acute period of repression of the church occurred in 1969-1970, immediately after Medellín. When Nelson Rockefeller made his report to President Nixon on Latin America after "his riot-punctuated hemispheric overview" in 1969, he listed the church among the "forces for change," saying:

> Truly, the church can be in a similar position to young people: with a deep idealism but, as a consequence, in some cases vulnerable to subversive penetration; ready to undertake a revolution, if necessary, to end injustice, but not clear either as to the ultimate nature of the revolution itself or as to the governmental system by which the justice it seeks can be realized.

Despite Rockefeller's paternalistic overtones, comparing the church to idealistic, vulnerable and unclear youth, he was recognizing the fact that the church was "a force dedicated to change" and that its support of the powers that be could no longer be taken for granted. The church had discovered the poor and—like God in the Bible—was siding with them.

"The Voice of the Voiceless"

In an atmosphere of spiraling repression the church is becoming more and more "the voice of the voiceless." In many cases it is the only voice. A young Dominican jailed in Brazil launched the following anguished appeal to his church for help just after his attempted suicide:

> The hope of prisoners is in the church, the only Brazilian institution outside the military control of the state. Her mission is to defend and promote human dignity. Wherever there is someone suffering it is the Master who suffers. The hour has come when before it is too late, our bishops must say, 'Enough!' in face of the tortures and the injustices which the regime is using. The church must not be guilty of sins of omission. We carry the proofs of the tortures in our bodies. If the church does not set her face against this situation, who will? In a time like the present, silence is a sin of omission. The spoken word is a risk but still more it is a witness. The church has to exist as the sign and the sacrament of the justice of God in the world.[11]

"Enough" by Solōn.

The Church has been that kind of sign during this "long night of terror." Sometimes with a low voice and a low profile, in long anonymous dealings with authorities and officers it is pleading for prisoners, being an advocate for people and groups; supporting their families, feeding thousands of unemployed; building bridges of tolerance or understanding, or obtaining a last-minute pardon or a quick exile to save a life. On other occasions it is publicly denouncing torture and injustice, analyzing the situation in serious documents; gathering data and preparing dossiers for international institutions for the defense of human rights. Along with such denunciation it is announcing the gospel of hope and liberation, as if saying with the Lord of the church, "Revive and lift up your head because the time of your liberation is at hand" (Luke 21:28).

Whether a low voice or loud and clear, anonymously or publicly, by word or by action, by denunciation or announcing hope, the prophetic witness is always costly.

The Church of the Martyrs

During this long decade the church has become again the church of the martyrs.

One of the first victims of this repression of Christian witness was Monsignor Helder Camara's secretary *Father Antonio Henrique Neto,* who was savagely murdered on May 26, 1969, in the city of Recife. He worked with youth, particularly with students, but probably his assassination resulted from an intimidating campaign against the Archbishop of Recife.[12]

Sometimes the brutal reaction happened precisely because these Christian ministers were pleading for or defending the defenseless. *Father Rodolfo Lunkenbein* in Matto Grosso, Brazil, was killed by big landowners while he was with Indians of the area, although there was no violent provocation by any of them. *Father Joao Bosco Penido Bournier,* a Jesuit missionary, went to the police station with Bishop Pedro Casaldaliga, in the same state of Matto Grosso, to plead for two peasant women who were being tortured and whose cries were heard all over the place. He was insulted and slapped in the presence of the Bishop, hit in the face with a revolver and killed with a dum-dum bullet.[13] The people of the town, including the tortured women, later on raised a cross where Father Joao Bosco was murdered and with their own hands destroyed the jail doors. They decided to raise a temple in memory of Father Joao Bosco in the same place, but the police would not hear of it and twice destroyed the memorial cross. Bishop Casaldaliga said, "It doesn't matter. The church will be built in some other place. What matters is that the church is built on martyrs' blood. . . ."

Other times the killing had no relation at all to the actions of the victims, but was only for vengeance or intimidation. Priests become the target of para-military or para-police rightist groups. Such was the case of *Fathers Duffau, Kelly* and *Leaden* and *Seminarians Barletti* and *Barbeito,* who were found assassinated in their parish in Buenos Aires, Argentina, the day after an admiral's daughter was killed in her home by a bomb placed by a terrorist organization. The five victims had nothing to do with the terrorist action.

The same happened in El Salvador, where the right-wing terrorist organization Union Guerrera Blanca (White Warriors Union) assassinated *Father Alfonso Navarro,* "an energetic parish priest who had been working with peasant and labor groups," in revenge for the killing of the Foreign Minister Mauricio Borgonovo Pohl on May 11, 1977, by the *Fuerzas Populares Liberación* (Popular Forces of Liberation).[14]

The terrorist White Warriors Union gave an ultimatum to the 50 Jesuits in El Salvador to leave the country or be killed. The Jesuits stayed, saying, "We are going to continue to be faithful in our mission until we fulfill our duty or are liquidated." It is precisely because of the church's identification with the impoverished and harassed people of El Salvador, particularly the poor peasants, that Jesuits and other priests, including *Archbishop Oscar Arnulfo Romero,* are the target for the ire of the dominant group in that little Central American country.[15]

Puebla: The Cry Resounds Again

During the last two years of preparation for the Third Conference of CELAM the pending question was: Would Puebla confirm and develop Medellín or would it outdo it? There has been both underground and open struggling between the progressive and conservative sectors of the Roman Catholic Church. The General Secretary of CELAM, Monsignor Alfonso Opez Trujillo, a known conservative and enemy of liberation theology, had tremendous power to influence and freedom to manipulate during that time. The Vatican had the power to appoint a considerable number of members to the conference, putting more weight on the conservative side. The Pope's influence had a moderating effect. The organization of the conference was such that the bishops were isolated behind what was called the "velvet curtain." They were kept away from the press and from the liberation theologians. Gary McEoin and others like him were denied press credentials. But the bishops found ways to get in touch with one or the other, and even "Women for Dialogue" were able to get to the bishops with their message. The influence of "progressive bishops" like Helder Camara and Paulo Evaristo Arns from Brazil, Leonidas Proaño from Ecuador, and D. Oscar Romero from El Salvador was apparent.

The Puebla Conference took a middle-of-the-road stance. There was no endorsement of liberation theology, as some radicals might have wished, but there was no condemnation either, as others wanted. There was a strong articulation of the classical Catholic doctrinal structures, but the prophetic line was also strong. Violence was rejected and priests were not encouraged to become directly politically involved, but denunciation of injustice and repression and the call to Christian participation in society were reinforced. A balanced concept of liberation received a definite sanction from Paul VI's Apostolic Exhortation on Evangelization, which was the basic text on which to discuss the theme of "evangelization in Latin America today and in the future." The *Comunidades de Base* (small grass-roots Christian communities) received their official consecration. And the "option for the poor" came out loud and clear. In one word, Medellín was confirmed.[16]

"The cry of my people," the cry of the poor in Latin America, crossed the "velvet curtain" and prevailed over all the schemes to keep Puebla in a spiritual and institutional aseptic atmosphere. The cry heard at Medellín, amplified by 10 years of painful struggles with the poor and in behalf of the oppressed, was heard again.

> From the bosom of the different countries of the continent a tumultuous and impressive cry is going up to heaven with increasing power. This is the cry of a people suffering and demanding justice, freedom, respect for the most elementary rights of persons and peoples.
>
> The Medellín Conference already pointed, a little more than ten years ago, to the acknowledgement of this fact: 'A contained cry springs from millions of people, asking from their pastors for a liberation which doesn't come from anywhere.'
>
> The cry might have seemed muffled at that time. But now it is clear, increasing, impetuous, and at times threatening.
>
> Our mission of taking God to people and people to God implies as well the building up of a more fraternal society.[17]

The cry of the poor was heard in the context of the scandalous and contradictory situation of Latin American society, with its increasing gap between rich and poor. So the hearing was translated into denunciation:

> We see in the light of the faith, as a scandal and a contradiction of what it means to be Christian, the increasing gap between rich and poor. . . . The wealth of the few becomes an insult to the misery of the great masses. This is contrary to the plan of the Creator and to the dignity of the human person. In the people's pain and anxiety, the church discerns a situation of social sin, of a magnitude all the greater because it takes place in countries which call themselves Catholic and which have the capacity to change. . . .

Preferential Option for the Poor

The bishops were clear about their "preferential option for the poor" but they were not exclusivistic or simplistic in their understanding of the poor. Brooding over the document—the composite work of 21 commissions—one is impressed by the well-rounded articulation of the concept of the poor, biblically grounded and directly related to the present situation of Latin America:

> The vast majority of our sisters and brethren still live in a situation of poverty and even aggravating misery. The poor lack not only material goods, but also social and political participation. They are made in God's image and they are the object of God's predilection. The Church takes for them a preferential option, very special but not exclusive or excluding. And this commitment to the poor—a sign of evangelical authenticity—demands the conversion of the whole Church in view of their total liberation. The Church in many sectors and places has made more real and it has deepened its commitment to the poor, in prophetic denunciation and service, bringing about many times tensions and conflicts, persecution and vexations, even death. But not all Christians or churches have engaged in this witness, solidarity and service to the poor.[18]

The doctrinal reflection of the document gives the biblical foundation for such a preferential option for the poor:

The evangelical commitment of the Church, as the Pope said, must be like Christ's—an engagement with the poorest (Luke 4:18-21). The Son of God showed this commitment in becoming human, identifying himself with the people, becoming one of them and assuming the situation in which they were—in his life, and, above all, in his passion and death where he reached the maximum expression of poverty.

By this only reason, poor deserve the preferential attention, whatever their moral or personal situation may be. Made in God's image to become his children, this image had been darkened and even scorned. Thus God takes their defense and loves them. This is why the poor are the first addressees of mission and their evangelization is *par excellence* the sign of the mission of Jesus.[19]

This option for the poor has to be shown in the church itself becoming poor; in Christians adopting a simple style of life ("evangelical poverty") in solidarity with the materially poor; and in cooperating with other churches and people of good will "to eradicate poverty and to create a more just and fraternal world."

Evangelization Today and Tomorrow

We must remember that all this concern of Puebla for the poor is in the context of the over-all concern with evangelization. The Bishops of the Northeast of Brazil in their preparatory document boldly affirmed: "To assume the situation of the poor is the necessary condition to understand the Gospel as good news." This affirmation became the basic axiom at Puebla, linking inextricably evangelization and the poor: "The preferential option for the poor has as its aim the annunciation of Christ the Savior." How is this so? What is the rationale for this striking declaration?

The poor are the first addressees of mission—in Jesus and in His Church. And the poor have also a potential for evangelization, because they question the Church constantly, calling her to conversion, and because many of them carry out in their lives the evangelical values of solidarity, service, simplicity and availability to receive God's gift.

In coming near to the poor to accompany and serve him or her, we are doing what Jesus taught us, when he became our brother, poor as we are. Consequently, our service to the poor is the privileged criterion, though not exclusive, of our following of Christ. The best service to our brother or sister is evangelization which prepares him or her to become children of God, to liberate them from injustices and promote their whole human life.[20]

When Puebla elaborates on evangelization, we Protestants—who are so committed to evangelization and consider it our fundamental vocation—would do well to listen. The Puebla interpretation of evangelization is thoroughly holistic, in the context of the Gospel, in the scope of evangelization (to evangelize the poor, the elite, youth, the family, the church, culture, popular religiosity, etc.) and in the methodology of evangelization.

Particularly significant and revealing is the characterization of the family and the *Comunidades de Base* (small grass-root communities) as adequate agents for evangelization. The fundamental concepts are taken from Pope Paul VI's Apostolic Exhortation *Evangelii Nuntiandi,* but the analysis of the Latin American context for evangelization and the incarnation of the Gospel in our situation is something unique.

There is something, however, that worries ecumenically-minded Protestants and Catholics, and this is the Marian emphasis (including popular piety around Mary's images and sanctuaries), boosted by the Pope and picked up by the conference, and the scanty references to the ecumenical dimension of the mission of the church in today's Latin America. The Pope's visit and public projection—with his undeniable human quality and sympathy—have contributed, paradoxically, to a reinforcement of the more traditional, institutional, and Roman aspects of Latin American Catholicism. Though we hope that the dynamic reality of Catholicism in Latin America goes beyond the Pope's understanding and expectations, what we have said above is something to reckon with for our mission in the '80s in Latin America.

Paradoxically, it may mean that we need to be both more Protestant and more ecumenical in our witness in Latin America! For the future of Latin America we Protestants should be more ecumenically oriented. For the sake of the Roman Catholic Church—her renewal and recovery of the evangelical dimension in her mission—we need to be better Protestants and evangelicals in our witness. Here lies the root of our commitment to mission in Latin America.

In relation to this we can understand the importance of the Oaxtepec Assembly of churches.

Oaxtepec: The Latin American Council of Churches

The ecumenical movement in Latin America has a long and rich history, beginning with the Panama Congress in 1916. Some of the national councils of churches, such as Mexico's, are more than half a century old. In 1941 the Latin American Evangelical Youth Conference (ULAJE) pioneered, in the region and in the world, a memorable continental congress where some of the most outstanding Latin American leaders were introduced to the international ecumenical scene. As we have said before, the Latin American Evangelical Conference met three times (in Buenos Aires in 1949, in Huampani in 1961, in Buenos Aires in 1969) and brought together a wide range of Protestants of the continent to reflect on the meaning of the evangelical presence and mission in our continent.

We have already mentioned the task-oriented ecumenical groups such as ISAL, CELADEC, MEC, MISUR, who made a substantial contribution to ecumenical witness and reflection. We have not mentioned other groups and activities, such as the four regional Associations of Theological Schools or the Latin American Congress on Evangelism (CLADE), or Evangelism-in-Depth, which brought together almost all the Protestant churches in several countries.

But in all these manifestations of Christian union and cooperation, we never came close to constituting a Latin American Council of Churches. In 1963 UNELAM was created as a Provisional Commission for Evangelical Union in Latin America, under the creative leadership of Pastor Emilio Castro of Uruguay, the present Director of the Commission on World Mission and Evangelism (CWME) in Geneva. For 15 years UNELAM was paving the way toward a closer and more organic cooperation among Latin American Protestants, through the direct participation of affiliated churches and councils and by sponsoring consultations and workshops on areas of common interest for the churches. Finally, Oaxtepec was the fruit of this long history of hopeful and agonizing search of the Latin American churches. Maybe it was, as well, a sign of the times.

From September 19-26, 1978, 110 churches and 10 ecumenical bodies met at Oaxtepec, Mexico. The representation was significant: 24 percent were Lutheran churches from several countries; 25 percent were representatives of various Pentecostal churches; 17 percent were Methodist national churches, and the rest represented other denominations. Some were newly created by Evangelical groups, such as the Latin American Center of Pastoral Studies (CELEP) and the Latin American Evangelical Theological Fraternity. The latter became members of the Executive Committee elected in the Assembly.

The Assembly dealt with two fundamental issues of Christian unity and Christian mission in Latin America. The areas covering the Latin

American context for mission showed the present generation's new awareness and wide scope of interest. The decision to create the Latin American Council of Churches (CLAI) was approved, and it now passes—through the elected Executive Committee—to the churches for action and implementation.

One of the most outstanding facts of the Oaxtepec Assembly was the constant reference to "the poor" in all the documents which came from the 10 discussion groups. Some have found that the Oaxtepec Assembly was even more specific and clear on this point than the Puebla conference. Be that as it may, the fact is that the Evangelical (meaning Protestant) churches of Latin America are beginning to hear loud and clear "the cry of my people."

As a historical landmark, as a pointer to the future, and as a sign of hope, we would like to close this chapter on the Latin American churches with the letter from the Oaxtepec Assembly.

Oaxtepec, Mexico
September 26, 1978.

LETTER TO CHRISTIAN CHURCHES AND TO INTERDENOMINATIONAL BODIES OF LATIN AMERICA

Greetings in the name of our Lord Jesus Christ.

We, the representatives of one hundred and ten different churches and ten ecumenical bodies of the whole continent, being aware of the wish of our Lord that we be one, and being alert to the challenge and demands of this hour, we have met as brothers and sisters to reflect, in the light of the Scriptures, on our common vocation and to make concrete our longing for unity.

In this Assembly we have discovered anew that our unity is a reflection of, and a participation in the unity of love from the Father, the Son and the Holy Spirit. We have prayed and sung together. We have come together to the Lord's Table and we have shared the experience of joy and pain of our brethren. We have discussed, warmly and frankly, the complex subjects that have to do with the life and mission of the Church in our continent. We have heard again the urgent call to the integral (holistic) proclamation of the Gospel. We have recognized that the Church is inserted in a reality which shows the consequences of sin and that it participates in this reality. We have been challenged to look for the King of the Kingdom in the midst of great contradictions and the poignant needs of our peoples.

We confess that we have dishonored God with our divisions, our pride, and our disobedience to Him. We confess that our indifference to the cry of the most forgotten, most oppressed and most needy sectors of our countries is a contradiction to the demands of the Gospel. We confess that we have not always been listening to the voice of our Lord, claiming us to take solidarian and efficacious actions in favor of those who suffer.

We make a joint call to Christians in Latin America to respond to the demands of the justice of the Kingdom in an obedient and radical discipleship.

We wish to communicate that, together with the penetrating Bible study on the unity theme, the delegates to the Latin America Assembly of Churches have studied and analyzed several subjects which reflect the set of problems of our peoples. We point to some of them to share with you our deep concern.

POWER STRUCTURES: When we face the evils which affect our peoples, we face not only individual sin but truly demonic powers of oppression and dehumanization entrenched in economic, political, social and ideological structures. The economic dependence that impoverishes our peoples and impedes their development, the injustices which marginalize whole sectors of the people and which concentrate power in small groups, the repression that falls upon some populations and sectors of our peoples, are some of the manifestations of this situation.

As Christians, who believe in That One who has conquered the powers of evil, who is the source of any authentic authority and of any genuine power, we pledge ourselves to fight for the transformation of all those structures, so they may fulfill the service for which they have been created.

FORGOTTEN SECTORS: The marginalization suffered by great sectors of society, such as children, youth, senior people and women, attempts against the dignity of human beings who have been created "in God's image and likeness." The Church has the obligation to propitiate the full self-fulfillment of each one of the members of society.

ABORIGINAL POPULATION: The situation of the indigenous people presents to us a disheartening picture which hits our consciences: usurpation of the Indians' lands, neglect by the governmental institutions, exploitation and discrimination. The Church is summoned to co-participate in the solution of these problems.

MINISTRY TO THE BROKENHEARTED AND THE DEFENSE OF LIFE: A ministry to victims of any type of violation of human rights is very urgent: to the disappeared and their families, to political prisoners, refugees and those who suffer repression.

DEFENSE OF ECOLOGY: The irresponsible exploitation of nonrenewable natural resources destroys the biological balance and attempts against the well-being of this and future generations. The Church must raise consciousness of the ecological problem and it must denounce specific cases of environmental contamination.

THE SITUATION IN NICARAGUA: The extreme situation through which the Nicaraguan people are passing at this moment calls us to Christian solidarity with those who suffer violence and repression and who live the tragedy of their broken rights. (This was written before the collapse of the Somoza dynasty; later on CLAI called the churches to a bold participation in the reconstruction of the nation of Nicaragua.)

CLAI—IN FORMATION: The Latin American Assembly of Churches, recognizing the Lord Jesus Christ as its God and Savior according to the Scriptures, and considering its common vocation, has established the basis for the creation of a Latin American Council of Churches. In order to consolidate our unity and to constitute itself as a useful instrument for the fulfilling of our mission, we have elaborated the juridical and operational basis for this body. It is our hope that, in the process of formation, in which local churches will participate, the Holy Spirit will call the churches and ecumenical bodies of the continent to incorporate themselves to the Council, which will become the visible expression of our union.

The favor of the Lord Jesus, Messiah, the Love of God and the solidarity of the Holy Spirit be with all of you.

fraternally,

THE DELEGATES AND THE ASSEMBLY OF CHURCHES OF LATIN AMERICA

7

OUT OF CAPTIVITY
The Theology of Liberation

What we have been describing in former chapters may look like a situation of captivity. And it is. "The cry of my people" is the cry of the captives. Yet this book does not intend to be gloomy or negative. "The cry of my people" is a cry of hope.

Out of captivity the Christian churches are coming to new life and new dimensions of mission. Out of captivity a new way of being Christian and a new style of life and spirituality are in the making. And out of captivity a new theology and a new way of doing theology has been born—the theology of liberation. It is the first truly Latin American theology ever.[1]

When we speak of "liberation" or "theology of liberation" some Christian brothers and sisters become scared. They immediately have in mind scenes of violence and visions of guerrillas and terrorism, like that artist who was asked to illustrate the cover of our book *Salvation Is Liberation*. He did not read the book, of course, which was trying to present to the churches, in a stimulating and acceptable way, the new reflections on the mission of the church coming from the World Conference on Mission and Evangelization in Bangkok in 1973. He just related in his mind the two words "salvation" and "liberation" and drew a picture of an angel with a gun! Of course, he had missed the whole point.

Some others just "turn on" with the word "liberation," and they will buy the whole package under that label. Though we must recognize that through indiscriminate, promotional, and superficial use of the word, it becomes first inflationary and, finally, devaluated.

We should begin then, by remembering that "liberation" is a fundamental biblical concept, through and through. It has been recovered through the present experience of Latin American

Christians—out of captivity, in a biblical way: the Liberator God is known in the situation of captivity and through the historical experience of oppression.

Liberation: A Biblical Concept

The liberation theme runs like a golden thread through the whole Bible, from Exodus to the cross and the Resurrection; from the Jewish Passover to the Christian Passover; from historical liberation in the life of Israel to the personal and communitarian liberation of the Christian community; from the groaning of creation to the eschatological liberation of the Kingdom of God. Jesus' name is the name of the Liberator: Joshua, which means literally in Hebrew "God liberates."

It is a fact, pointed out by biblical scholars, that Israel knew God first as the Liberator in her history, before she recognized Him as the Creator of the Universe. The God of Israel, the God of the Exodus, is the God of liberation, the Liberator of the slaves and oppressed. He is the God of the Prophets, the Holy One of Isaiah who comforts the exiles and uses Cyrus the Emperor as his servant, who opens new doors and builds a highway for the return of the expatriates. He is the Liberator God of the Virgin Mary in the Magnificat, a God who

has shown strength with his arm,
has scattered the proud in the imagination of their hearts,
Has put down the mighty from their thrones,
and exalted those of low degree;
he has filled the hungry with good things,
and the rich he has sent empty away. . . . (Luke 1:51-53)

Jesus himself uses a messianic promise from Isaiah to introduce himself as the Liberator, anointed by God:

The Spirit of the Lord is upon me,
because he has anointed me to proclaim good news to the poor.
He has sent me to proclaim release to the captives
and recovering of sight to the blind,
to liberate those who are oppressed
to proclaim the acceptable year of the Lord. (Luke 4:18-19)

After a long history of the spiritualization of these words from the Gospel, a few scholars and interpreters are beginning to unpack the dynamite of this passage.[2] It began in the context of the Jubilee Year proclamation, which required periodic restructuring of society, the return of the land to landless families, the emancipation of slaves, and the cancellation of debts. (Exodus 23:10-11; Leviticus 25; Deuteronomy 15:18; Isaiah 61:1; Jeremiah 34:8; 34:13-17; Ezekiel 46:17).

Liberation belongs to the language of salvation, both in the Old and the New Testament. Other related words are *redemption* and *remission,* used both for the emancipation of slaves and for the inner liberation of the forgiveness of sins. *Salvation* in the Old Testament has a sense of *deliverance,* pointing to the concept of liberation. Now if Paul was using freely the word "redemption," and other similar words, to announce the saving work of Christ, is it improper to use "liberation" today to announce the full Gospel of Jesus Christ?

But the theology of Liberation in Latin America was not born merely out of a theoretical meditation of the biblical theme of liberation; it came out of the experience of oppression and biblical reflection in the context of "dependence" and "domination."

Theology from the Experience of Oppression

James Cone, the black American theologian, reminds us that the theology of liberation is the theology of the oppressed. This is true of any liberation theology (black, feminine, Latin American, South African, or any other). It was natural for the black slaves in America to identify with the story of the slaves in Egypt and their liberation, coming back once and again to that fundamental core (fundamental for Israel's faith and also for the Christian slaves) in their worship, their preaching, and their singing: "Let my people go," "Go down, Moses," "Oh what a morning!" They were projecting their liberation to the future, to the crossing of the Jordan, to heaven, to a future Kingdom where there would be no slaves and the poor and oppressed would be walking free, in white robes, singing joyfully in the city of Jerusalem. All those biblical images, says Cone, were not merely opium for the slaves; they were instead expressing the black affirmation of their humanness, their hope that "somewhere," "somehow," "someday" justice would be done and they would be free.[3] In the '60s the descendants of the slaves, led by Martin Luther King and others, began to demand that justice and freedom "now."

Many Christians in Latin America were caught up also by this gospel of liberation from the Bible, and they began to realize that in the Bible this liberation is something that happens in history. They also shared in the hope of a better world, one "more just and more human" (a sort of Latin American dream), but they began to see that the Liberating God was already working and walking in history to liberate the people, and that they were called to join God in the struggles for human liberation today.

The theology of liberation was not the product of seminary professors working at their desks but the reflection of Christians engaged in human struggles. It was the result of a new reading of the Scriptures in a particular historical situation. It was not an intellectual exercise but a participation in the story, the story of God's liberating action in history. The experience of the Exodus became the key to a new perception of the Gospel, as the bishops viewed it at the Medellín Conference:

> As Israel in the old times, the first people, were experiment-ing the saving presence of God, when He made them cross the Red Sea and guided them toward the Promised Land so we also today, the New People of God, cannot but feel the passing, for each one of us and for all, from less human conditions to more human conditions of life.

The Exodus became not only a memory of the community of faith but an experience and a hope. The Word became incarnate. The reading of the Bible was a dynamic relationship between text and context, the Bible and reality were blended together. As a Colombian lay theologian said; "We have to read Latin material with the eyes of the Bible, and we have to read the Bible with the eyes of Latin America".

It was during the '60s, the "decade of development," and after the bitter disillusionment with that scheme, that an avant-garde of Christians began to think and speak and act in terms of "liberation." The Medellín conference gave the initial thrust to this new theological reflection and this new reading of the Scriptures:

> It is God himself who, in the fullness of time, sends his Son in the flesh, to come and to liberate all men from all the captivities of sin, ignorance, hunger, misery and oppression, in one word, injustice and hate, originated in human egotism.

The seeds of the new theology were already there. The biblical concept of liberation had been recaptured for the proclamation of the Gospel, for the historical task of a Christian generation, and for new theological reflection. Medellín became a point of arrival after a long process, and a departure point for a hopeful generation.

Let us hear Gustavo Gutiérrez, a Jesuit priest from Peru and one of the most influential theologians of this new group, testify about the experience of his generation.

The Itinerary of a Christian Generation

Gustavo Gutiérrez describes what he calls the "itinerary of a Christian generation" that led to the discovery and emergence of a new way of doing theology.

1. We started, he says, in a stage of *unawareness* and political indifference. We Christians had a dualistic view of the world, divided into the religious and secular spheres. This world is only the stage for the next, this life is only a rehearsal of the true life to come. In this way religion and the church become the spiritual accompaniment of the status quo.

2. Then we moved into a stage of *awareness* of the existence of social problems: poverty, malnutrition, illiteracy, marginality and injustice. In this stage we tried to apply some Christian principles ("Christian humanism") through social programs of development or through political parties of Christian inspiration.

3. This generation realized the limitations of the above reformist approach and entered into an accelerated *process of radicalization,* moving towards a revolutionary stance. We went beyond our former impressionistic description of the evils of society to a deeper structural analysis, going straight to the roots of our socioeconomic problems and all their different ramifications. We saw that violence, oppression and repression are part and parcel of the system. This new understanding coincides with the revolutionary movements throughout Latin America that in the '60s were attempting to change the system.

4. At this point "the major event in our generation" took place: the *discovery of the world of the "other,"* namely, the neighbor—the nearby neighbor and the distant neighbor in oppressed classes, races or nations. And with this discovery of the world of the other came the option for the poor, in whom Christ meets us.

This is, as we saw in chapter one, *a truly evangelical conversion: to Christ in the neighbor.* From here on, says the Peruvian theologian, comes a new way of being Christian, a new style of life, and a new way of doing theology.[4]

The Man on the Road

Sergio Torres, a Chilean priest exiled in the United States, tells the same story in a different way, the parable of the Good Samaritan: There was—and there is—a man on the road. Today in Latin America he is multiplied by millions who are like him, beaten, stripped, half-dead, on the road. And we, as Christians, need to fulfill the command of our Lord: "Go and do likewise." So we tried to help the man on the road.

First, we started with direct beneficent assistance programs: we fed him, found jobs for him, helped his children get into school, and so on.

Then, we discovered that this was not enough: we needed more structured and scientific programs. It was the time of "development programs," sponsored by European and American development agencies and churches. We brought experts, models and studies, on projects involving housing, education, rural development, cooperatives, and so forth.

Then came the "conscientization" approach: It is not a question of providing services for people but helping them to help themselves, to stimulate consciousness-raising helping them to organize themselves, to produce their own "cultural revolution."

Finally we realized that we were dealing with social, political and economic structures, that even "conscientization" of the people wasn't enough. We discovered that poverty is not a given fact or something that happens, but a product of our society (which produces the rich and the poor at the same time). Those structures are favoring the national oligarchies and the international economic and financial powers. So we had to enter into socioeconomic analysis, using the scientific and ideological tools available, and join the common struggle to change those structures.

Finally, we left behind the development ideology and came to the liberation concept. We discovered that it was right there in the Bible. We began to reflect on the liberating Word of God from the context of our captivity. To help the man on the road we had to engage in the liberation struggle to change society, and to do so from our Christian faith, believing in a liberating God working through history.

Protestant Theologians

As we have seen in the former chapter, Protestants have been following a parallel itinerary in their discovery of society and their search for an incarnational theology. The Argentine theologian

Beatriz Melano Couch, describing the evolution of Protestant theology in Latin America, finds three stages:

1) The *crisis of liberalism* in the 1950s: "the social gospel and the ideals of democracy and personal freedom became inadequate to cope with unjust and oppressive structures on our continent."
2) The *awakening of reflexive consciousness* in the 1960's: a new kind of social awareness and an effort to overcome the pietistic individualism and otherworldliness inherited from the *revival,* by means of a theology of development, ecumenically oriented, but still not realizing the real situation of Latin American "dependence."
3) The *creative commitment to change* in the 1970s, a theology "born on the road," with a certain feeling of euphoria and the vision of a "humanistic socialism" for Latin America. It was a time of hope for liberation and the building up of "a new man and a new society."[5]

Rubem Alves, a Presbyterian theologian from Brazil, was the "prophet" of liberation theology in his book *A Theology of Human Hope.*[6] It was his doctoral dissertation, a dialogue with contemporary theologians and philosophers. In it Alves was trying to articulate in theological language the voices of the poor and oppressed, both in the Third and the First worlds (the black, the poor, the young). He rejects the theology of Bultmann, Barth and Moltmann insofar as these great contemporary theologians do not take seriously enough the world, history and human action. Humanity has a vocation for freedom and is moved by hope, and so Christians must engage in the struggles for liberation against the cultural, political and technological forces that keep history captive.

Theology of the Exodus . . . and the Exile

In the early '70s Rubem Alves was working on a theology of the Exodus. For him the Exodus was not merely an episode in the past but the structuring center of the biblical faith, "a paradigm for the interpretation of other historical situations." The human person is *homo viator,* the pilgrim or migrant, and the Exodus represents the possibility of breaking with the past, the release from captivity, suffering and oppression. Exodus means exit, migration. To migrate means to get out of a social structure which has exhausted its possibilities and is repressive and hopeless into a different one, based on freedom, because "without freedom, life is not real life." But this Exodus, this exit, this migration, is not programmed by the dominant social structure. It demands decision, imagination, and action.

Alves' next book was inscribed in the situation of captivity. The optimism of former years was gone. Political liberation movements had been crushed. Repression was rampant. It was also written in English with the suggestive title *Tomorrow's Child*. It is not yet time for liberation. Alves was one of the first theologians to realize this fact. It is the time of waiting for tomorrow's child. What is the basis of our present hope? What is the meaning of captivity? What can we do for liberation from our situation of oppression? Alves' answer is that we have only God's creative act (in the past) as the foundation for our hope, as in Habakkuk's prayer (3:17). Oppression and repression have not the last word. History is pregnant. But it is not yet the time for childbirth. Captivity and exile may last a long time, but in the meantime we have a task, as Jeremiah told the captives in Babylon (Ch. 29). There is the political task of sowing, of conceiving the new future. It is the time to incarnate that future in the community of faith. Only the oppressed can be creative, because they have the will to change the power and inertia of oppression. The Bible tells us that the task of the captives (as in the Old Testament exiles and in the New Testament emergent Church) is to create the counter-culture! In doing that, in living by hope in the coming liberation, we can love and we can celebrate. We already have the first signs, the *aperitif* of the Kingdom, we can feel the movements in the womb of tomorrow's child.

The other Protestant writer who dominates the decade, together with Alves, is the Methodist theologian from Argentina, José Miguez-Bonino, former observer at the Vatican II Council and one of the presidents of the World Council of Churches. While Alves is more a philosopher, Miguez-Bonino is the ethicist. His theme is the Kingdom and his leitmotif is love, incarnate love, mediated in history through human solidarity and commitment to the oppressed. José Miguez-Bonino has been for many years an engaged critic, participating from inside the church and ecumenical movements. His books and articles show a solid biblical and theological foundation. Dr. Miguez is equally respected and accepted by Protestant, Catholic and radical evangelical theologians, though his option for the theology of liberation and a socialist project for Latin America is perfectly clear. His latest work, *Christians and Marxists: The Mutual Challenge to Revolution,** is "probably the clearest and most thorough confrontation between Marxist ideology and Christian faith that has been produced so far," according to Beatriz Melano Couch.

---

* London, Hoddes and Stoughton, 1976.

Theology from Praxis: What in the World Is This?

By this time we must be willing to ask a question about the meaning of theology and of liberation. Gustavo Gutiérrez, the most systematic exponent of this theology, defines theology as "the critical reflection on the liberating praxis of Christians."

And what is *praxis?* It is a Greek word which means *practice.* But in contemporary philosophical and ideological discussion it means a dynamic interaction between theory and practice, between action and reflection. Theory has to be tested by practice, and practice has to be corrected by theory. Knowledge doesn't come merely by intellectual exercise, but out of experience, out of engagement. This is, after all, what the Bible says about truth and faith. Truth is not only apprehended, as the Greeks believed, *truth has to be done.* "To know God," according to the prophets, is *to do* justice, to have mercy, to do his will (Jeremiah 22:13-16; 9:23; Hosea 4:1-6; 6:6). Jesus invited people not to believe certain doctrines or accept certain ideas but to follow him. "Those who want *to do* the will of God *will know* if my doctrine comes from God." Truth is done, truth is known on the way, through engaged obedience. This is Christian praxis. Jesus summarizes the point in a very striking way in John's version: "This is the condemnation: that the light came to the world, but the world rejected the light because their deeds (Greek: *praxis*) were evil." So, according to your praxis will be your faith, your knowledge, your relationship to Christ. This is why the theologians of liberation are saying that what should concern us is not *orthodoxy* (right belief) but *orthopraxis* (right action-reflection).

As we have seen in earlier chapters, thousands of Christians have been engaged in the last years in trying to do God's will in the Latin American situation of oppression, joining other people in the struggle for human liberation at many levels. Liberating acts are the first and most important thing. The theology of liberation comes as "a second moment," as the "critical reflection on the liberating praxis of Christians." But, as Gustavo Gutiérrez says, "one thousand thoughts on liberation are not worth one single act of liberation."

And What is Liberation?

In the second chapter of *A Theology of Liberation*, Gustavo Gutiérrez describes the process of liberation as he understands it, in three interpenetrating levels or approaches:

1. In the first place, *liberation* expresses the *aspirations* of *oppressed peoples* and social classes, emphasizing the conflictual aspect of the economic, social and political process which put them at odds with wealthy nations and oppressive classes.

2. At a deeper level, *liberation* can be applied to an *understanding of history.* Man is seen as assuming conscious responsibility for his/her own destiny. In this perspective the unfolding of all man's dimensions is demanded—a man who makes himself throughout history. The gradual conquest of true freedom leads to the creation of a new man and a qualitatively different society. . . .

3. Finally . . . the word *liberation* allows for another approach leading to biblical sources. . . . In the Bible, Christ is presented as the one who brings us liberation. Christ the Savior *liberates man from sin,* which is the ultimate root of all disruption of friendship and of all injustice and oppression. Christ makes man truly free, that is to say, he enables man to live in communion with him; and this is the basis for all human brotherhood.

1. Let us look at the first level. Liberation begins as a human *aspiration* and it takes shape in the *struggles* of the oppressed peoples against what oppresses them. In the Latin American situation it is the struggle for economic, social and political justice. We can easily deduce that in other situations it may be the struggle against racial, sexual, spiritual or cultural oppression. The painful experience of the last two decades in Latin America has shown to many economists, sociologists, politicians and concerned Christians that the basic fact is *dependence and domination.* Christians share with other human beings the situation of oppression and dependence; they share the aspirations for liberation, and a growing number of Christians are sharing the above analysis and theory and the subsequent commitment to the struggle for human liberation.

Of course, these aspirations and struggles are not exclusive to the Third World or Latin America. As Gutiérrez says:

What is at stake in the South as well as in the North, in the West as in the East, on the periphery and in the center, is the possibility of enjoying a truly human existence, a free life, a dynamic liberty which is related to history as a conquest.

Proof of this is the awareness of new and subtle forms of oppression in the heart of advanced industrial societies, which often offer themselves as models to the underdeveloped countries. In them subversion does not appear as a protest against poverty, but rather against wealth.

The movements for a simpler style of life ("small is beautiful") and the various streams of "radical discipleship" in North America are good examples of this protest against wealth and consumerism and of the search for human liberation and "the quality of life."

2. At the second level, liberation appears as a *historical process of humanization.* Reviewing the history of the last four centuries, what emerges is the picture of a "dynamic and historical conception of man, oriented definitely and creatively towards his future," "taking hold of the reins of evolution." Although he warns that we have to look at this development of ideas critically, Gutiérrez holds that "history advances inexorably and demonstrates that the achievements of humanity are cumulative . . . in order to achieve an ever more total and complete fulfillment of the individual in solidarity with all humankind." In this process the human person is not looking only for "liberation from *exterior* pressures which prevent his fulfillment as a member of a certain social class, country, or society. He or she seeks likewise an *interior* liberation, in an individual and intimate dimension." He or she seeks liberation not only on a social plane but also in a psychological one. Liberation, for Gutiérrez, is multidimensional and it is a continuous process. The vision is no less than a new person in a new society.

> The goal is not only better human conditions, radical change of structures and social revolution; it is much more: the continuous creation, never ending, of a new way of being human, a permanent cultural revolution.

This naturally brings us to the third level of liberation.

3. Liberation at the third level is liberation *from sin.* This is the "radical liberation" because sin is the root of all oppressions, both in its individual and social dimensions.

Positively speaking, this radical liberation is the gift which Christ offers us: communion with God and with other people.

This liberation is final and as such must be eschatological.

Yet it has to happen in history. Though it is a gift, it is also human action. One level of liberation cannot take place without the others, Gutiérrez insists; it is only one salvific process on three levels.

Following Gutiérrez' reasoning in other chapters of his dense book, it becomes clear that the first level corresponds to *action* (particularly political action, ruled by rationality, where Christians work with the same tools as non-Christians in society); the second level is the level of *utopia* (an intermediate level between faith and action); and the third level is the level of *faith,* the level of theology.

At this point it must be clear to all of us that what Gutiérrez calls liberation is nothing else than salvation.

Salvation in History

The Peruvian theologian defines salvation simply as "the communion of people with God and the communion of people among themselves." To be saved is to be open to God and to others. True liberation—or salvation—means to be liberated *from* oppression and *for* others. We are liberated to love. This is the way to understand Paul's assertion, "For freedom Christ has set us free" (Gal. 5:1). We go from liberation to freedom, from freedom to communion.

> The freedom to which we are called presupposes the going out of oneself, the breaking down of our selfishness and of all the structures that support our selfishness; the foundation of this freedom is openness to others.

By the same token, "to sin is to refuse to love one's neighbor and, therefore, the Lord himself." Sin is the closing in of oneself, and negation or the destruction of a truly human community in God.

But both sin and salvation are "intrahistorical realities"; they take place in history. Sin, for instance,

> . . . is regarded as a social, historical fact, the absence of brotherhood and love in relationship among men, the breach of friendship with God and with other men, and therefore, an interior, personal fracture. . . . Sin is evident in oppressive structures, in the exploitation of man by man, in the domination and slavery of peoples, races and social classes. Sin appears, therefore, as the fundamental alienation, the root of a situation of injustice and exploitation.

Salvation works in history, since the very beginning, in Creation— "the first salvific act." The human person was put on earth to be a co-creator, a collaborator with God in this salvific process. The *Exodus* is the paradigm of a salvation, a liberation, that is working in

'Where will the hope come from?" by Solon.

history, including political liberation but open eschatologically to a total liberation in human brotherhood, in communion with God. God made a covenant with Israel and a new covenant in Jesus Christ, both in history and with the purpose of transforming history. God's promise unfolds through history. God's salvation "orients, transforms and guides history to its fulfillment." God wants to encounter the human person in history and, according to the biblical story, every human person becomes God's temple. Every neighbor becomes the meeting place with God and Christ.

The center of this salvific process in history is Jesus Christ, the Lord of history, the Liberator. Christ irreversibly assumed the human situation in the Incarnation and "irreversibly committed himself to human history." "By his death and resurrection he redeems man from sin and all its consequences." Christ is walking and working in history, orienting, transforming and leading the process to its fulfillment.

There is only *one history:* "the history of salvation is the very heart of human history, but not apart from it." There is only one call, one vocation, and one convocation to all human persons: communion with God through grace. "There is no one who is not invited to communion with the Lord, no one who is not affected by grace." In fact, grace is present—whether accepted or rejected—in all men and women. For this reason "we can no longer speak of a profane world." We accept or reject God's salvation through what we do in relation to human liberation. "Human existence, after all, is nothing but a yes or no to the Lord."

Christian Spirituality

It is clear that for Gutiérrez, both Christians and non-Christians are participating in this salvific, liberating process in history. But Christians are doing it out of their faith and commitment to Christ. *Christian* existence becomes a passover, a sharing with Christ in his cross and resurrection. This is the heart of Christian spirituality of liberation. This means that we face the conflictual character of history and cast our lot with those with whom Christ identified himself. There is "a paschal core of Christian existence and of all human life; the passage from the old man to the new, from sin to grace, from slavery to freedom."

This *paschal spirituality* is one of the most challenging traits of many Christians in Latin America today, engaged in the struggles for human liberation, according to their particular vocation and in the most diverse situations. Some of them are working with cooperatives in rural areas; some conducting grass-roots community groups, centered in the Bible and in the situations people are living in; some of them are being the "voice of the voiceless," defending the human rights of city workers, of peasants expelled from the land, or students confined to jail. Some of these Christians are supporting the struggles for human dignity and liberation through the structures of the church, through official declarations or denunciations, through public or private advocacy, through serious analysis of the social situation and the exploration of alternatives. Others choose personal involvement, as leaders or simply as members of all kinds of movements. Some are even joining revolutionary movements, attempting to trigger change through guerrilla action. And both the nonviolent and those who have resorted to violence as an ultimate option are putting their lives on the line for this commitment to human liberation.

For these Christians, liberation is not something they are looking for for themselves, but for all. Their liberation will come with the liberation of all. They have been liberated—in their new understanding of faith—to give themselves to and to participate in, the struggles in spite of all the ambiguities of historical action. Their liberation has more of the crucifixion than of the resurrection. But they are moved by the "power of the resurrection," the only basis of hope for a "new heaven and a new earth," a new person and a new society. They know that there are no blueprints, no short cuts, no maps. There is no resurrection without crucifixion. But there is a promise of the resurrected one: "I will go ahead of you . . . where there are two or three gathered in my name, there I will be. . . . I am with you always to the end of the world."

"My Life for My Friends"

Let us share with you an account of one of these Christians, a young Bolivian university student who became engaged in the guerrilla movement in his country: Néstor Paz Zamora.

Néstor belonged to an old well-to-do Catholic family of Bolivia. His father was a general in the Bolivian army who had held very important positions in the Bolivian government. Néstor studied in a Jesuit school and went to Chile to start seminary training. Later he decided to enter the University of La Paz to pursue medical studies. He was active in the church and in society. One of his jobs was to teach religion in high school. He married a charming young girl from one of the respected families of Bolivia, and together they worked among the poor while living in a very simple home they made for themselves with adobe.

Néstor was also active in politics, both as a member of the Christian Democratic Party and in university politics, which in Latin American universities used to be a real school of politics and a force at the front line of social struggles. He was influenced by Ché Guevara, the Argentine-Cuban guerrilla leader, and by Camilo Torres, the Colombian priest who joined the guerrillas and died in his first encounter. He was, first of all, a committed Christian, an eager reader of the prophets and the New Testament. He absorbed the new ideas emerging from the circles of Christians committed to social struggle and led by progressive priests. The concept of liberation already was incorporated into his thinking, into his style of life, into his discussions and actions, even before the first book on liberation theology was written.

One day, two years after Ché Guevara's death in the first Bolivian guerrilla movement, he and 50 other university students decided to go to the mountains and start a new guerrilla movement. He said in his proclamation:

> 'Greater love has no man than this, that a man lay down his life for his friends. This is the commandment which sums up the "Law".'

> That is why we take up arms: to defend the illiterate and undernourished majority from exploitation by a minority and to give back his dignity to the dehumanized person.

> We know that violence is painful, because we feel in our own flesh the violent repression of the established disorder. But we are determined to liberate man because we consider him as a *brother*. We are the people in arms. . . .

> We have chosen this method because it is the only one open to us, painful though it may be.

After quoting Camilo Torres on "efficacious love" and "revolution," Néstor Paz goes on:

> I think that the only efficacious way of protecting the poor against their present exploitation is by taking up arms. I believe that fighting for liberation is rooted in the prophetic line of Salvation-history.[7]

So you see, the basic concepts of the theology of liberation are right here in this proclamation of a young student in his 20's. His journal and his letters to God and to his young wife are a moving testimony of his deep spirituality, what Gutiérrez would call the spirituality of liberation. He writes tender letters to his wife in his small diary. Remembering the family, birthdays, meals they used to have together, longing for favorite simple dishes while eating only roots or a little portion of canned food, longing for her presence, dreaming of having their own baby, sharing with her the experiences of the column in the jungle, celebrating the finding of a New Testament.

Let us finish with his letter to God, written a few days before his death:

> Dear Lord:
>
> It has been a long time since I wrote to you. Today I feel a real need for you and your presence, perhaps because of the nearness of death or the relative failure of the struggle. You know that I have tried to be faithful to you—always and by all means—consistent with my whole being. That is why I am here. I understand love as the urgency of helping to solve the problems of the "other person"—in whom you are present.
>
> I left what I had and came here. Perhaps today is my Thursday and tonight my Friday. (A reference to Maundy Thursday and Good Friday.) Because I love you I surrender everything I am into your hands, without limit. What hurts me is the thought of leaving those I most love—Cecy and my family—and perhaps not being here to participate in the triumph of the people—their liberation.
>
> We are a group full of true "Christian" humanity and I think we will change the course of history. The thought of this comforts me. I love you and I give you myself and ourselves, completely, because you are my Father. No one's death is meaningless if his life has been charged with significance; and I believe this has been true of us, here.
>
> Chau, Lord! Perhaps until that heaven of yours, that new world we desire so much!

Néstor Paz Zamora was concerned that he might not be here to participate in the liberation of the people. He wasn't. He died of starvation at noon on October 8, 1970. The struggle for liberation in his land still has a long way to go.

Was he right? Was he wrong? The guerrilla movement was a failure. They were massacred. Some, like Néstor, died of starvation. A handful were able to benefit from a late amnesty and flew to Chile. Nobody knows where they are now. Some would say that the guerrilla strategy was wrong. Some would say that the moment was wrong. Some would say that violence is not Christian or evangelical. Some would say that Néstor and his friends were misguided idealists, moved by illusion. Some may think they were suicides. All that may be true, or maybe not. God has the final word.

It seems to us that Néstor was right in the one thing that matters: that the center of Christian faith is love. Love understood as commitment to human liberation, as entering in the life of the "other" and working together for God's Kingdom of love and human friendship. Right or wrong in his final and specific option, we believe he had found the secret of Christian life and death when he was able to write, "No one's death is meaningless if his life has been charged with significance."

His short life was one fully charged with significance, like an arrow moving from liberation to communion in love. His last poem was, "To love is to die for your friends."

Néstor Paz' final cry before dying in the jungle is also part of "the cry of my people." It is a cry of love, solidarity and commitment to human liberation—and it is done in the name of Christ.

Shall we join in the Christian passover? No less than this—suffering, dying and rising with Christ in the neighbor—is necessary if we are serious about awareness, identification and responsible action.

Notes

Preface
[1]*Illusion and Reality in Inter-American Relations,* United Presbyterian Church in the U.S.A., Philadelphia, 1969.
[2]Catholic Bishops N. E. of Brazil, *I Have Heard the Cry of My People,* New York, IDOC North America, Summer 1973.

Chapter One
[1]Gustavo Gutiérrez, *A Theology of Liberation,* Maryknoll, New York, Orbis Books, 1973, p. 195 ff.
[2]Severino Croatto, "Popular Religiosity: An Attempt at Problematization," *Cristianismo y Sociedad* (Buenos Aires), April 1976, p. 42.
[3]José Miguez-Bonino, *Doing Theology in a Revolutionary Situation,* Philadelphia, Fortress Press, 1975, pp. 4-18.
[4]William R. Read, Victor M. Monterroso, Herman A. Johnson, *Latin American Church Growth,* Grand Rapids, William B. Eerdmans Publishing Co., 1969, pp. 27-35.
[5]Christian Lalive d'Epinay, *The Haven of the Masses,* London, Lutterworth Press, 1969.
[6]Germán Arciniegas, *Latin America—A Cultural History,* New York, Alfred A. Knopf, 1968, p. 17 ff.
[7]Lewis Hanke, *South America,* Princeton, New Jersey, D. Van Nostrand Co., Inc., 1959, p. 9.
[8]P. Bigo, *The Church and Third World Revolution,* Maryknoll, New York, Orbis Books, 1978.
[9]Emile G. Leonard, *O Protestantismo Brasileño,* São Paulo, ASTE, 1963, p. 747.
[10]Federico Debuyst, *La Poblacion en America Latina,* Madrid, Feros, 1961, p. 317.
[11]John J. Johnson, "The Emergence of the Middle Sectors," in *Latin American Politics,* ed. by Robert O. Tomasek, Garden City, New York, Doubleday, 1966, pp. 169-196.

Chapter Two
[1]John M. Crewdson, "Border Region Is Almost a Country Unto Itself, Neither Mexican Nor American," *The New York Times,* February 14, 1979, p. A22.
[2]Karl M. Schmitt, *Mexico and the United States, 1821-1973,* New York, John Wiley and Sons, Inc., 1974.
[3]Carey McWilliams, *North From Mexico,* New York, Greenwood Press, 1968, Chapters VI-IX, pp. 98-205.
[4]E. J. Williams, "Oil in Mexico-United States Relations: A Contextual Analysis and Bargaining Scenario," Tucson, Arizona, University of Arizona, mimeographed edition, © 1977, p. 10.
[5]John Ehrlichman, "Mexican Aliens Aren't a Problem . . They're a Solution," *Esquire,* August 1979, pp. 54-64.

[6]Jorge Prieto, "The Challenge of the U.S.-Mexico Border," *The Christian Century*, Vol. 95, No. 43, December 27, 1978, pp. 1258-62.

[7]Gregory Bergman, "Human Rights Fenced Out," *The Christian Century*, Vol. 95, No. 43, December 27, 1978, pp. 1265-67.

[8]David McCullough, *The Path Between the Seas*, New York, Simon & Schuster, Inc., 1977, p. 250.

[9]McCullough, p. 121.

[10]McCullough, p. 341.

[11]McCullough, p. 385 ff.

[12]McCullough, pp. 392, 397.

[13]David Perkins, *Hands Off—A History of the Monroe Doctrine*, Boston, Little, Brown & Co., 1941.

[14]Herbert L. Matthews, ed., *The United States and Latin America*, Englewood Cliffs, N.J., Prentice-Hall, Inc., 1964, p. 124ff.; Michael Elmer, in Edward L. Cleary, *Shaping a New World—An Orientation to Latin America*, Maryknoll, New York, Orbis Books, 1970, p. 220 ff.

[15]Cleary, p. 221 ff.

[16]Matthews, p. 221 ff.; Wade Crawford Barclay, *The Great Good Neighbor Policy*, Chicago-New York, Willet, Clark Co., 1945, p. 2.

[17]Irving L. Horowitz, Josué de Castro, John Gerassi, eds., *Latin American Radicalism*, New York, Vintage Books, 1969, pp. 63-68.

Chapter Three

[1]Gary McEoin, *Revolution Next Door*, New York, Holt, Rinehart and Winston, 1971, p. 1.

[2]Richard R. Fagen, "Studying Latin American Politics: Some Implications of a Dependence Approach," *Latin American Research Review*, 12, Vol. 2, July 1977, pp. 3-26.

[3]Eduardo Galeano, *The Open Veins of Latin America: Five Centuries of Pillage of a Continent*, New York, Monthly Review Press, 1974, p. 12.

[4]Galeano, p. 66 ff., p. 114 ff.

[5]Galeano, p. 66 ff., p. 114 ff.

[6]Dr. Neftalí Garciá, "Puerto Rico's Colonial Economy in the 20th Century: Preliminary Notes," Hato Rey, Puerto Rico: Mision Industrial de Puerto Rico, May 1975, pp. 1-17.

[7]Victor Sánchez-Cardona, Tomás Morales-Cardona and Pier Luigi Caldari, "The Struggle for Puerto Rico," *Environment*, Vol. 17, No. 4, June 1975, pp. 35-40; Hato Rey, Puerto Rico, reprinted article on "How to Undevelop an Island."

[8]Alvaro de Boer, O. P., "The Catholic Church in Puerto Rico: An Impression," mimeographed edition, San Juan, Puerto Rico, 1978, p. 15.

[9]Catholic Bishops of N. E. Brazil, "I Have Heard the Cry of My People," IDOC-North America, Summer 1973.

[10]Theotonio dos Santos, "The Crisis of the Brazilian Miracle," Working Paper, Brazilian Studies, Latin American Research Unit (LARU), Toronto, Canada, April 1977, p. 13.

[11]Celso Furtado, "El modelo brasileño," *El Trimestre Económico*, Vol. XL (5), Julio-Septiembre de 1973, No. 159; Estrategia No. 27, Marzo-Abril de 1974, Buenos Aires; *Cuadernos de Cristianismo y Sociedad*, Año 1, No. 3, Julio de 1974, Buenos Aires.

[12]Kurt Rudolf Mirow, *A Dictadura dos Carteis, Anatomia de Subdesenvolvimento,* Rio de Janeiro, Civilização Brasileira, 1978, p. 59 ff.

[13]Michael Harrington, *The Vast Majority: A Journey to the World's Poor,* New York, Simon & Schuster, 1977. Excerpts by the author in "Why Poor Nations Stay Poor, 'The Development of Underdevelopment,' " *Christianity & Crisis,* Vol. 37, No. 15, October 3, 1977, p. 21.

[14]Harrington, *loc. cit.,* p. 217.

[15]Harrington, p. 217.

Chapter Four

[1]"DINA'S Children: A Verdict in the Letelier Case." *Time,* February 26, 1979.

[2]*Presencia,* La Paz, Bolivia, cables from AP and IPS, December 9 and 10, 1978.

[3]Dorothee Sölle, "To Love Means Not To Hide," *The Christian Century,* Vol. 95, No. 28, September 13, 1978, pp. 824-828

[4]Sölle, pp. 824-828

[5]McEoin, p. 184ff.

[6]McEoin, p. 184ff.

[7]McEoin, p. 184ff.

[8]Charles Antoine, *Church and Power in Brazil,* Maryknoll, New York, Orbis Books, 1973.

[9]*Repression of the Church in Brazil* (title translated from Spanish), CEDI, Rio de Janeiro, December 1978. (Spanish version: *Cuadernos de Cristianismo y Sociedad,* Nos. 35-36, Buenos Aires, July-August 1979, pp. 13-48.

[10]*La Masacre del Valle,* Comisión Justicia y Paz, La Paz, 1974, mimeographed edition.

[11]Joseph Comblin, *A Ideologia da Seguranca Nacional,* Rio de Janeiro, Civilização Brasileira, 1970, p. 197 ff. Gavras made a film of Mitrione's story—"State of Siege."

[12]*Catholic Agitator,* Los Angeles, April 1976. The letter was received in February 1976.

[13]*Le Monde Diplomatique,* September 1977.

[14]Elaine Magalis, "Murder in Argentina," *The Christian Century,* Vol. 94, November 9, 1977, pp. 1030-1033.

[15]See House International Relations Subcommittee Hearings, U.S. Congress, 1976-77.

[16]*Ibid.*

[17]*America Latina: Derechos Humanos,* No. 3, Mexico: Cencos, A.C., 1977, pp. 8-15.

[18]*America Latina: Derechos Humanos,* No. 3, p. 89ff.

[19]Gabriel Garciá Marquez, *Alternativa,* Bogota, September 12-19, 1977, p. 16ff. Quoted in Documentos-3, *Prisa,* San Juan de Puerto Rico, n.d.

[20]*La Razón,* Buenos Aires, June 12, 1976.

[21]*Contacto,* diciembre 1976, p. 21.

[22]Comblin, p. 197ff.

[23]See A. M. Schlesinger, *The Imperial Presidency,* Boston, Houghton Mifflin Co., 1973; Richard Smoke, *The National Security Affairs* (Vol. 8, *International Politics,* of *The Handbook of Political Science,* ed. by Fred I. Greenstein and Nelson W. Polsby, Reading, Mass., Addison-Wesley, 1975.

pp. 247-362); Robert Borosage, "The Making of the National Security State," in *The Pentagon Watchers*, Garden City, New York, Doubleday, 1970; R. Aron, *Imperial Republic: The United States and the World, 1945-1973*, Englewood Cliffs, New Jersey, Prentice–Hall 1974.
²⁴R. Barnet, *Roots of War*, New York, Penguin Books, Inc., 1973.

Chapter Five
¹Friedrich Engels, *Origin of the Family: Private Property and the State*, New York, Pathfinder Press of New York, 1972.
²*Si me permiten hablar . . .*, Noema Viezzer, ed., Mexico, Siglo XXI 1977, pp. 216-230. *Let Me Speak*, New York, Monthly Review, 1978.
³*Ibid.*
⁴Dorothee Sölle, *op. cit.*
⁵Wilson T. Boots, "Four Women Confront a Nation," *Christianity & Crisis*, May 1, 1978.
⁶"Machismo—Creole Style," Washington, D.C., LADOC, June 1975, pp. 12-19.
⁷Germaine Tillion, *Le Harem et les Cousins.*
⁸Mario Montaño Marañon. "Patriarcado v Matriarcado en la Sociedad Chola," *El Pais Machista*, La Paz, 1977, pp. 194-200.

Chapter Six
¹Orlando E. Costas, *Theology of the Crossroads in Contemporary Latin America*, Amsterdam, Rodopi, 1976, Ch. 4, pp. 86-102.
²*Deudores al Mundo*, UNELAM, Montevideo, Uruguay, 1969.
³*Ecumenical Review*, July 1970; Emilio Castro, *Amidst Revolution*, Belfast, Christian Journals Limited, 1975, pp. 80-99.
⁴John Eagleson, ed., *Christians and Socialism*, Maryknoll, New York, Orbis Books, 1975.
⁵See "Evangelism and the World" by René Padilla, "Evangelism and Man's Search for Freedom, Justice and Fulfillment" by Samuel Escobar, and "Response to Lausanne" or "Theology and Implications of Radical Discipleship" in *Let the Earth Hear His Voice*, ed. by J. D. Douglas, Minneapolis, World Wide Publications, 1975, pp. 116-146; 303-326; 1294-1298. See also the publications of the Latin American Theological Fraternity, *Fe Cristiana y America Latina Hoy* and *El Reino de Dios y la Historia.*
⁶José Comblin, "Medellín: Problemas de Interpretación," in PASOS, No. 24, 20 de agosto de 1973, p. 3.
⁷Segundo Galilea, *Reflexiones sobre la Evangelización*, Quito, IPLA No. 10, 1970. John Drury, *Between Honesty and Hope*, New York, Maryknoll Books, 1969.
⁸Helder Camara, *The Spiral of Violence*, Denville, New Jersey, Dimension Books, 1971.
⁹"Conclusions," *The Church in the Present-Day Transformation of Latin America*, Washington, D.C., U.S. Catholic Conference, 1970, Vol. II, 2:16, 14.
¹⁰Dean Peerman, "CELAM III: Measured Steps Forward," *The Christian Century*, Vol. 96, No. 12, April 4, 1979, pp. 373-8.

[11]Charles Antoine, *Church and Power in Brazil,* New York, Orbis Books, 1973, pp. 7, 266.

[12]Antoine, p. 242 ff.

[13]D. Pedro Casaldaliga, *Creio Na Justica e na Esperanca,* Rio de Janeiro, Civilização Brasileira, 1978, pp. 128-138.

[14]"El Salvador: The People Versus the Government," Report by the Unitarian Universalist Service Committee made after an investigation January 7-12, 1978.

[15]*Persecución de la Iglesia en El Salvador* ("Persecution, Occasion for Witness"), Paul Philibiana, Proaño, CEI, Rio de Janeiro, Documento 87, September 1978.

[16]Dean Peerman, "CELAM III: Measured Steps Forward," *The Christian Century,* Vol. 96, No. 12, April 14, 1979, pp. 373-8.

[17]Puebla Documents Nos. 87-90.

[18]Puebla Documents Nos. 28, 87-90, 383, 707, 733, 769, 1134-1140.

[19]Puebla Documents Nos. 1141-1152.

[20]Puebla Documents Nos. 1130, 1142, 1141-1165.

Chapter Seven

[1]For North American assessments of this theology, see *Theology in the Americas,* ed. by Sergio Torres and John Eagleson, Maryknoll, New York, Orbis Books, 1976; Robert McAfee Brown, *Theology in a New Key: Responding to Liberation Themes,* Philadelphia, Westminster Press, 1978.

Latin American basic works are: Gustavo Gutiérrez, *A Theology of Liberation,* Maryknoll, New York, Orbis Books, 1973; Juan Luis Segundo, *The Liberation of Theology,* Maryknoll, New York, Orbis Books, 1977.

See "Introductions" to *The Latin American Theology of Liberation* by Jose Miguez-Bonino, *Doing Theology in a Revolutionary Situation,* Philadelphia, Fortress Press, 1975; Hugo Assman, *A Theology for a Nomad Church,* Maryknoll, New York, Orbis Books, 1976.

[2]Paul Gregorios, "To Proclaim Liberation," in *To Set at Liberty the Oppressed,* ed. by Richard D. N. Dikinson, Geneva, World Council of Churches, 1975, pp. 186-193. John H. Yoder, *The Politics of Jesus,* Grand Rapids, William B. Eerdmans Publishing Co., 1972.

[3]James Cone, *God of the Oppressed,* New York, Seabury Press, 1975. See also Letty Russell, *Human Liberation in a Feminine Perspective,* Philadelphia, Westminster Press, 1974.

[4]Gustavo Gutiérrez, *Praxis of Liberation and Christian Faith,* San Antonio Texas, Mexican-American Cultural Center, 1974. See also *Living with Change, Experience and Faith,* ed. by A. Eigo, Villanova, Pennsylvania, Villanova University Press, 1976.

[5]Beatriz Melano Couch, "New Visions of the Church in Latin America: A Protestant View," in *The Emergent Gospel,* ed. by Sergio Torres and Virginia Fabella, Maryknoll, New York, Orbis Books, 1978.

[6]Rubem Alves, *A Theology of Human Hope,* New York, Corpus Books, 1969.

[7]Nestor Paz Zamora, *My Life for My Friends,* trans. and ed. by Ed Garcia and John Eagleson, New York, Orbis Books, 1975.